© Cynthia McFarland/Stabenfeldt
Original title: Western Riding
© Photos: Bob Langrish
© Photo of Cynthia McFarland, back cover: Steve Floethe

Stabenfeldt AS, 2009
Printed in Italy
Editor: Bobbie Chase

ISBN: 978-1-934983-25-6

Stabenfeldt, Inc.
225 Park Avenue South
New York, NY 10003
www.pony4kids.com

Available exclusively through PONY.

Western Riding

By Cynthia McFarland

Contents

Special thanks to all the riders and their horses who appear in this book. Much appreciation goes out to Tori Turbyfill; Ryan Samko; Laurel Samko; Dalton Brown; Dallas Brown; Jordan Smith; Jamie Bourque; Brooke Meisel; Cheyanne Meisel; Wyatt Pogue; Cade Pogue; Ashtin Geiger, and Madison Hurm. A heartfelt thank you to instructor/trainer Kelly Saylor for bringing the riders together, and to trainer Charlie Smith. You all did an amazing job!

Welcome to the world of Western riding!

As you'll quickly discover, it's not just ranch cowboys who ride in Western tack. Western riding has gained in popularity around the world and one reason is that there are so many different events. This means there's sure to be one (or more!) you'll enjoy.

Do you love to ride fast? If so, barrel racing or pole bending might be exactly what you're looking for. Do you have a pretty horse with smooth, even gaits and a lovely way of going? You might like to enter him in Western pleasure classes to see how you compare with other exhibitors.

Trail classes offer unique challenges as you and your horse have to negotiate a variety of different obstacles. If the cowboy life holds a special place in your heart, cutting is a great way to experience one of the tasks that working cowboys do all the time. Cutting a single cow out of the herd and keeping her from returning might sound simple, but it takes a talented horse to do the job with style and grace.

If you want to test your ability as a rider, Western horsemanship is a great opportunity. Your horsemanship skills will be put to good use as you guide your horse through this pattern class. Reining competitions showcase the talent of the horse as he performs a variety of maneuvers, and a tough reining class brings out the best in each horse and rider team.

Many horse owners appreciate the chance to show their horses in halter and showmanship classes. You won't be riding your horse in these classes, but it still takes plenty of practice and skill to win.

Whatever event you decide to participate in, you'll want to feel comfortable and confident in your basic riding and horse handling abilities. Find a knowledgeable trainer who can help you master the basics and then advance to learning the intricacies of a particular event.

Of course, you don't have to ever set foot in a show arena to enjoy riding Western. Many riders find that Western tack has the most comfortable saddle to use when trail riding. You can spend many happy hours exploring new trails and terrain on your horse. Those may be some of the best times you share with your four-legged partner. Trail riding is definitely when I have the most fun with my Paint horse, Ben.

Ready to get started? Read on to learn more about these exciting and challenging Western events!

1. The Basics

As you're about to discover, there are many Western riding disciplines that you can enjoy with your horse.

If you want to show your horse, youth classes are for junior exhibitors under the age of 18. Youth classes are divided into divisions by age, so you might have a class with ages 10 and under, a class for 12 and under, and a class for ages 13 through 17. They may also be broken down by ages differently.

If you ride in a breed show, whatever breed that may be, the rules for that particular association will apply. You should have an up-to-date rule book for your breed so you know what equipment is allowed and how the judges will score each class.

Some breeds and types of horses are better suited to Western riding than others. In jumping and English riding, riders often choose warmbloods or horses with Thoroughbred bloodlines. For Western events, the stock horse breeds are most popular, although any horse can be ridden in Western tack. Some of the more common breeds you will find competing in Western classes include the American Quarter Horse, Paint Horse, Appaloosa, and color breeds, such as the Palomino, Buckskin, and Pinto. Arabians, Morgans, Tennessee Walking Horses, and many other breeds also compete in Western events.

When you are showing in a breed show as a youth or amateur (someone who hasn't been paid to train, ride, show or assist in training a horse), you must show registration papers proving you or a relative own the horse. This is to prevent a professional or trainer from showing a horse in these classes.

You certainly don't have to own a registered horse to show Western. Many crossbreed and grade horses excel in Western events. Sometimes horses with a mixture of bloodlines make the best riding horses, so don't feel that you have to own an expensive purebred.

The most important thing is to find a horse that suits you well and is a good match in personality and ability. For example, if you want to compete in Western pleasure classes, you'll want an attractive, quiet horse with a lovely way of going. If your goal is to ride in speed events like barrel racing or pole bending, your horse must be fast, agile and responsive. A rider who competes in trail classes will want to have a sensible, calm horse, yet one who is bold and not easily intimidated. Certain bloodlines are naturally talented at events like cutting and reining.

The horse's size is also important because you want to present a pleasing picture in the show ring, no matter what class you are in. You won't look right if you are very tall riding a pony or small horse, or if you are quite small and have an extremely large horse. Being in the right proportion to your horse will also make it easier to control him.

You'll want a horse that is sensible and easy to load and unload in a horse trailer since you will be taking him to shows and competitions.

If you are a novice or beginning rider, it will be best to find an older, more experienced horse that can help you gain confidence. Don't make the mistake of buying a young, "green" horse that still needs a lot of training.

Never buy a horse based on looks alone! Sometimes a rider will have her heart set on finding a horse with a certain color or specific markings, but an incredibly beautiful horse isn't a good deal if he doesn't have the right temperament and training. You want a horse that is safe and will be a good partner.

It's important that your horse is good at loading and unloading into a trailer.

You'll want to have a trainer who has plenty of experience in the discipline you want to ride. That trainer may also be a good person to help you find just the right horse.

Before you begin to train for a certain discipline, you need to be solid in your riding basics. You should be comfortable and confident handling your horse on the ground and in the saddle.

On the ground, you should be able to lead, back, tie, groom, bathe and clip your horse. You should also be able to load and unload him into a horse trailer.

Position Matters!

In the saddle, you want to be able to ride confidently at all three gaits: walk, trot (jog), and canter (lope). Your body position has a great deal to do with how well you can control your horse. English riding instructors are very precise about position, and this is just as important when it comes to riding Western.

Sit upright on your seat bones, not back on the padded part of your bottom. You should sit centered in the middle of your saddle with your shoulders square with your horse's shoulders.

If you sit forward in the saddle, this encourages your horse to go faster. Many riders push back against the cantle (the back part of their saddle) when riding, but you should only sit far back in your saddle when asking your horse to stop. Riding too far back in the saddle all the time puts unnecessary weight right over your horse's kidneys and can make him sore.

Your legs should rest against the horse's sides and not be tight or pressing against him unless you are giving him a cue to do something. Don't hold onto your horse with your lower legs. This signals your horse to speed up and can also throw you off balance. Your grip should come from the knees up and you should use your lower legs only when cueing your horse.

When you are sitting in the saddle, someone watching from the side should be able to draw an imaginary line straight down from your shoulders, through your hips all the way to your heels. The front of your foot should be in the stirrup so that the ball of your foot rests directly on the stirrup with your heels down. This makes it easier to press your calf or heel against the horse's sides to cue him.

Don't push your feet into the stirrups and

Sit upright on your seat bones in the center of your saddle. This should be your position most of the time.

Don't ride far back in the saddle, as this puts too much weight over your horse's kidney area.

Instead, sit upright in the center of the saddle's seat.

Pushing your feet too far forward will move your body back in the saddle.

If your legs are too far back, your body will tilt forward.

ahead of your body. If your feet are too far forward this will push your body too far back into the saddle. If your legs are too far behind you, this will tilt your body forward. Either way, you'll be out of balance and have less control.

Hold the reins so that your hands are on top of the reins, not underneath. Your thumbs should be up, not horizontal.

If you always have tension on the reins, this can make your horse's mouth "hard" and he won't be as responsive to your commands. Have enough slack in the reins that you aren't pulling on them unless you are directing the horse to stop or turn. At the same time, you don't want to have so much slack in the reins that you can't gather them up quickly if you need to. You just want to maintain light contact with your horse's mouth, not a tight hold.

Whether you ride with one hand on the reins, or use both hands, you should have your hand(s) just above the saddle horn or pommel (front of the saddle) unless you are directing your horse with specific rein cues.

If you are riding a young horse and are using both hands on the reins, you will guide him the same way you would riding English. For example, if you want to turn to the right, your right rein is the active, guiding rein, and the left rein is "quiet" and just used for support.

If you are guiding your horse with one hand, as is common in many Western classes, he must know how to "neck rein." For example, when you want to turn right, you lay the left rein against the left side of the horse's neck and use your pressure from your left leg.

Many riders underestimate the importance of focus. You should keep your eyes focused ahead and looking in the direction you want to go. Just like driving a car, you want to

Hold the reins with your hands on top, not underneath.

look where you're headed. Avoid the temptation to look down.

Many times, a rider will look down to see what the horse is doing, but when you look down at the ground, this will throw you off balance. If you look down at your horse this can make him think he's doing something wrong. Instead your focus should be up and ahead in the direction you want to go. This will transfer to your horse and encourage him to go that direction.

In the show ring, looking up and ahead tells the judge that you are confident and in control.

Guiding & Cues

Many riders make the mistake of riding too much with their hands and not enough with their legs and seat. Your bottom half should always be doing more of the asking when it comes to communicating with your horse.

For example, if your horse is walking and you want him to trot, use your seat and legs to ask for increased speed. The movement of your hips in the saddle should urge the horse forward at the same time your calves squeeze against his sides.

Because you want your horse to remain sensitive to your legs, you don't want to maintain constant pressure on his sides. As soon as he responds, release the pressure from your calf. If you need to encourage him further, apply pressure again and then release it. If you constantly put pressure on the horse with your calves, he will be confused about what you are asking and can also start to resent your legs.

Even when you ask your horse to stop, your main cues should come from the bottom half of your body, not your hands. Don't just pull back on his mouth and expect him to stop. You want to prepare him by cueing him with your seat and legs first.

Stop moving your hips, which have been moving along in rhythm with the horse's movement. Exhale and let all your air out so you can sit deeply in the saddle. Slide back on the padded part of your bottom to the back of the saddle and keep your arms straight. You want to hold your hands in place to encourage him to stop, but don't just pull back on the horse's mouth. Keep your horse's head, neck and body straight, and always keep your shoulders in line with your horse's shoulders.

As you practice this method of stopping, you can begin making the cues subtler. Even reining horse riders who perform a dramatic sliding stop use this method.

Work on Maneuvers

There are many different maneuvers you can practice to improve your riding and control of your horse. Be patient with your horse and make sure he knows what you are asking him to do. Remember that horses

When leg yielding, your horse moves forward and sideways at the same time.

learn best when you break it down into small steps. You can't expect your horse to master something new in just one lesson.

Riding in circles, figure-eights and serpentines (a weaving "S" shape) will help your horse learn to bend and pay attention to your cues. You will have to use your seat, legs and hands to direct him through these maneuvers.

Your horse should know to yield away from your leg pressure, whether you are asking him to move left or right. He should move smoothly when you press your leg against his side. When leg yielding, your horse should continue moving forward, but also laterally (sideways) because of the pressure from your leg. For example, if you press his side with your right leg, he should continue to move forward and also laterally to the left at the same time. His front and hind legs should slightly cross over as he moves.

When your horse is two-tracking, he is moving forward and laterally, and in a diagonal direction. His front and back legs should step across. His body should be slightly bent opposite the direction he is moving. For example, if you are riding to the right, his body should be slightly bent to the left. This exercise helps polish your guiding and encourages the horse to yield to your legs. Riding along a fence or rail will help give your horse a boundary as you practice.

When you ask the horse to sidepass, he

When the horse is two-tracking, his body is slightly bent to the opposite of the direction he is moving. This horse is moving to the right, but his body has a slight bend to the left.

should move laterally with his front and back legs stepping across. Hold your hands still to keep him from moving forward, but don't turn his head in the direction you want to go. It's your seat and legs that push the horse sideways in whichever direction you want him to sidepass. His head, neck and body should remain straight the entire time.

It's much easier to start teaching the sidepass using a fence or wall as a direction. If your horse is facing the fence and you cue him with you right leg to move left, he can't go forward, and it's easier for him to understand you want him to sidepass to the left. As he learns, you can gradually move away from the fence.

As your horse sidepasses, his front and back legs step across since he is not moving forward, but just to the side.

Your horse should know about lead changes and how to pick up his left or right lead whenever you ask. When your horse is on the left lead, both his left front and left hind leg are moving forward farther than his right. The opposite is true when the horse is on the right lead.

A lot of riders don't realize the horse actually picks up the lead with his inside hind leg first. As that inside hind leg moves forward and picks up the lead, the front inside leg will follow. Use your seat and leg to cue the horse to pick up the correct lead. You literally push the horse into the correct lead by putting weight on your "outside" seat bone and pressing him with your "outside" leg. ("Outside" refers to the side on the rail, not the inside of the arena or circle in the direction you are traveling.)

When the horse has weight on his inside hind leg, this helps him pick up the correct lead. Some riders pull their horse's head to the inside in an attempt to make them pick up the correct lead, but this actually encourages the horse's hind end to move to the outside and makes it harder for him to pick up the correct lead. The horse's head should be straight, not turned to either side, when you ask him to lope.

When the horse's weight is on his "inside" hind leg, this helps him pick up the correct lead on the front.

Remember, if you make sure he is positioned to pick up the correct lead on the inside hind leg, then he will get it correct on the front end.

The counter canter is when your horse is loping (cantering) on the outside lead, instead of leading off with his inside legs. For example, when you are loping to the left, your horse's correct lead is his inside, or left, lead. But if you ask him for a counter canter, he would pick up the right, or outside lead, even though loping to the left. Practicing the counter canter can improve your horse's balance and strength. It will also improve your horse's lope, making it more rhythmic.

Short & Simple

It will help to think of your horse as a five- or six-year-old child. Nobody would expect a child in kindergarten to know how to read or do algebra. Those skills come later with much time and practice.

The same thing applies when you and your horse are learning new techniques. When you are teaching your horse a maneuver for the first time, ask your trainer to show you how to break it down into simple steps. As your horse learns each step in order, then you can ask for a little bit more.

Don't expect your horse to learn it all at once or you will both get frustrated. Keep your teaching sessions short, say 15 minutes or less. This doesn't mean you will only ride for 15 minutes at a time, but rather that you will only work on something new for short periods of time. After that, go back to doing something the horse already knows and

Make it a point to end on a positive note every time you ride. If you are trying to teach something new, don't end in the middle of the lesson. Finish working on this and then do something your horse knows well and stop after that. You want to end each session with your horse relaxed and confident. If you quit when either you or your horse is frustrated or upset, this will carry over to the next time you ride.

understands. Then you can continue to build on the new lesson.

Every time you ride your horse, you are teaching him, whether you know it or not. This is why it's important to always ride with correct position and to pay attention to what your body is telling your horse.

You shouldn't ride one way when you are practicing in the arena and then ride a completely different way when you are riding on the trail with your friends. Be consistent so your body and cues are always telling your horse the same thing, no matter where you are riding or what you're doing.

2. Tack & Equipment

Most people think of the American cowboy when they think of the Western saddle, but the saddle actually has a much older history. The origins of this style of saddle actually reach all the way back to the horseback warriors of the Dark Ages.

Long ago in the time of the knights and crusaders, saddles were designed with high forks and cantles to keep the rider securely seated during battles. The Spanish Conquistadors later modified this saddle and brought it with them to the Americas in the 1500s. Eventually the saddle they once used for war evolved into a stock saddle for working cattle. These early versions had no horn and the fork and cantle were both lower, while the stirrups were cut from a single piece of wood.

In North America, this Western stock saddle continued to be modified through the years. A horn was added, making it possible to rope and catch cattle. By the late 1880s, wood horns were being replaced by steel horns since wood horns had a tendency to break under the strain of roping cattle. Riggings, skirts, types of stirrups, and saddle decorations all varied depending on the area of the country. You could tell what part of the country a cowboy was from just by looking at his saddle. Cowboys in Texas usually had square skirts and double riggings on their saddles, while California cowboys preferred a rounded skirt.

Types of Western Saddles

Before you buy a Western saddle, you'll need to know what events and activities you plan to participate in, as some require different types of saddles. Let's look at a few saddles and what makes them different. Keep in mind that the fork is the front of the saddle, also known as the swell or pommel, while the cantle is the upright part of the seat at the back of the saddle.

Ranch/roping saddles are built for hard work and tend to be the heaviest of the Western saddles. They have a thick, stout horn that is wrapped for roping and a double rigging (front and back cinch) to help keep the saddle in place under the strain of tying cattle. Ranch saddles typically have a deep seat and a high cantle.

Reining saddles are built to put the rider in close contact with the horse with a low seat, thinner stirrup leathers and cutout skirts, all designed to make it easier for the rider to be closer to the horse. A reining saddle has forward hung stirrups that allow the rider to sit back and deep in the saddle during the hard stops and turns so common in the sport of reining. The horn and fork are of medium height. These saddles are not designed for the hard work of roping and ranch work and only have a front cinch.

Cutting saddles are easy to identify because of a tall, thin horn which the rider holds onto while competing. A flat seat and forward hung stirrups help the rider sit deep during the horse's active movements. The cantle is fairly low and the saddle has a double rigging to help keep it in place.

Barrel saddles are the smallest and most lightweight of the Western saddles, typically weighing under 30 pounds. They have a high fork, high cantle and deep seat to help the rider stay securely balanced during the sharp turns and high speeds necessary in the sport. The seat is made of rough-out leather to provide good grip and the skirt, whether rounded or square, is short. Barrel saddles have only a front cinch.

Pleasure/trail saddles are popular with many riders and come with a variety of seats, skirts and horn styles. They are made to be comfortable for hours of riding and may have a padded seat. They usually have a high fork, medium height cantle and rounded skirt to reduce their weight. These saddles are heavier than a barrel saddle, but lighter than a ranch/roping saddle. Stirrups are often wide and the saddle may have a double rigging. This is a good all-around style of saddle and popular with many riders.

Show saddles are, just as the name implies, designed for the show ring. Often highly

embellished with silver trim and leather tooling, the saddles typically have a good-sized skirt to show off these decorations. The seat is designed to help keep the rider balanced in the center of the saddle and is often padded suede. The horn is fairly short and the cantle is low.

The underside of every Western saddle has a sheepskin lining, which may be either natural or synthetic. This lining provides a layer of cushion to the horse's back and also helps keep the pad or blanket from slipping.

In every category, saddles can be fancy, plain or somewhere in-between. If you plan on showing, you'll probably want a saddle with a bit of decoration, such as silver work, stamped and carved leather or leather lacing.

If you buy a custom-made saddle from a saddle maker, the stamping and carving are done by hand and involve many hours of work. You can decide what kind of design and pattern you would like. On manufactured saddles, this work is done by machine. As you determine what kind of saddle you'll need, familiarize yourself with some common saddle terms so you'll be more knowledgeable when you start shopping.

Ranch/roping saddle

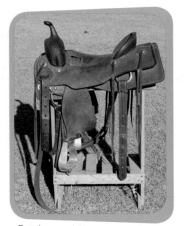

Cutting saddle

Reining saddle

Barrel saddle

Pleasure/trail saddle

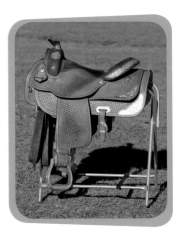

Show saddle

The saddle tree greatly determines how the saddle fits your horse. Saddle makers often use soft wood trees such as Ponderosa pine, ash, beechwood, cottonwood, etc., and then cover the form with rawhide. Some manufacturers are now using plastic and fiberglass to make synthetic saddle trees as they are less expensive than traditional wood.

Trees come in different sizes and this determines how well the saddle fits your horse's back. "Full-quarter horse bars" are wider than "regular-quarter horse bars," while "semi-quarter horse bars" fall in between these two widths. There are also "Arabian bars," which are designed to better fit the narrower build of Arabs and similar breeds.

A semi-quarter horse or full-quarter horse tree will fit the conformation of a majority of horses, but it's important that the saddle fits your horse properly. Have a horse professional help you check the fit.

A saddle with a single rigging has a front cinch only.

A saddle with a double rigging has both a front and back cinch.

A poor-fitting saddle can lead to many horse problems, including:

- Objection to being saddled
- Sensitivity to being brushed or touched in back area
- Tail swishing
- Pinning the ears
- Tossing the head
- Slow to warm up or relax
- Reluctance or refusal to change leads
- Lack of extension
- Excessive concussion or choppy movement
- Inability to use back and hindquarters properly
- Muscle atrophy or lack of development, despite exercise
- Uneven hoof wear
- Restriction of respiratory system

Rigging is a basic part of the saddle and refers to the arrangement that holds the latigos and cinches that keep the saddle on the horse. Saddle rigging is either single or double, meaning the saddle has either one front cinch (single rigging) or both a front and back cinch (double rigging).

Saddles designed for roping and ranch work, cutting, and trail riding are double-rigged to make them more stable and secure on the horse's back.

When you purchase a show, barrel or reining saddle, these are single-rigged and only have a front cinch.

Pay close attention to the seat because this plays a large role in how comfortable the saddle will be when you ride. For starters, you'll want to get the right size seat. The size of a saddle is determined by measuring the distance from the base of the horn to the top middle edge of the cantle. The smallest is 12 inches (youth), and sizes increase in half-inch increments up to 17 inches. Generally speaking, when you are sitting in the saddle, there should be about four inches between you and the fork, or the front of the saddle. Your bottom should be close to the base of the cantle, but not pushed back against it.

You want a saddle you feel comfortable in, and the slope, curve and basic construction of the seat will determine how the saddle feels. You will spend the majority of time in the lowest point of the seat, so look for a saddle that has a centered-seat to encourage proper riding position. You will probably end up trying out quite a few saddles to find one that is comfortable for you and fits your horse properly.

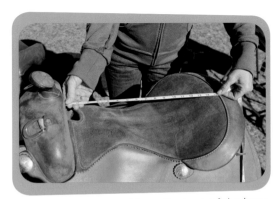

Saddle size is measured from the base of the horn to the top middle edge of the cantle.

With proper care, a quality, well-made saddle can last for decades. You'll want to protect your investment by taking good care of your saddle. Wipe it down with a soft cloth each time you finish riding. A few times a year you should also give it a thorough cleaning.

To do this, remove the cinch(es), stirrups, and any attachments. Use a clean sponge and saddle soap or glycerin bar with just enough water to make a good lather. You don't want to use much water because the leather will absorb it and it will take longer for the saddle to dry.

Wash all of the saddle, except for any rough-out or suede areas. (These areas should just be brushed for cleaning.) Use the sponge and soap to thoroughly clean both sides of the leather. Once you've done the entire saddle, use another sponge or soft rag dipped in clean warm water to go over the saddle, removing all traces of soap.

Let the saddle dry completely out of the sun. After the saddle is totally dry, you can apply a bit of leather conditioner or neatsfoot oil, if you like.

Saddle Pads & Cinches

Some people try to find a saddle pad to make their saddle fit the horse, but this is the wrong approach. Proper saddle fit should be your primary consideration; then you can buy the pad you like.

As you'll quickly find out when you visit the tack shop, there are many saddle pads and blankets to pick from in both natural fibers and synthetic materials. Natural fibers include pads/blankets made from wool, cotton, mohair, or combinations of these. Many horsemen prefer wool pads because they conform well to the horse's back, are long-lasting and absorb moisture. Navajo blankets are popular with many riders because they are 100% wool and come in a variety of attractive colors and patterns.

If your horse has high withers, he might benefit from a pad that has a cutaway section at the front. Some pads feature "wear leathers," which are pieces of leather along the edges in areas where the saddle may cause wear by rubbing.

Some people like to use a thin pad underneath and top this with a good saddle blanket. This will keep the blanket clean longer and provide more cushion under the saddle.

If you use a thin pad, you may want to top it with a saddle blanket.

When it comes to synthetics, you'll see pads made from neoprene, rubber, plastic, nylon and rayon. Some of these provide great cushion but can be hot on the horse's back. If you have questions about which pad is best for your horse, your trainer or instructor can give you advice.

Whichever pad you choose, make sure it extends out at least an inch on all sides of the saddle. You don't want the saddle itself sitting on the horse's back, but you also don't want an enormous amount of pad sticking out from under the saddle.

> Don't make the mistake of using too thick a pad or a combination of pads and blanket(s), as this can actually make your saddle less stable on the horse's back.

You'll need a good cinch, also known as a girth, to secure the saddle on your horse. Just like pads, cinches come in a variety of materials, both natural and synthetic. Many riders prefer a mohair cinch because it's strong and easy to clean. Cotton, rayon, nylon, felt and neoprene are also used to make cinches and have their advantages and disadvantages. For example, neoprene has good grip, but it generates heat and may rub horses with sensitive skin.

Cinch size is measured from the outside of one cinch ring to the other.

Cinches come in different sizes, and come in two-inch increments, ranging from 22 to 38 inches. This measurement is from the outside of one cinch ring to the other. There is a strip stitched across the center of the girth with small rings on it so you can attach a tie-down or breast collar. When properly adjusted the cinch should fit your horse so that this strip is in the middle of your horse's girth line, and the large end rings should each be about eight inches below the saddle rigging loops.

If you aren't sure what size girth you need, here's what you can do to get a good idea. Tie your horse up or have someone hold him still. Place your pad and saddle on the horse's back, and tie a piece of baling twine to the saddle rigging loop on one side. Bring the string under the horse's belly along the girth line where the cinch should rest and hold it up to the bottom of the other rigging ring.

Make a mark on the string where it meets the ring. Now take the string off the saddle and measure it. Then deduct 16 from that number and you'll have a close estimate of the correct cinch size. If you come up with an odd number, round up to the next number. For example, if you get 31 inches, round up to 32 inches and buy that size cinch.

Rings on cinches can be made of stainless steel, bronze, nickel or chrome-plated metal. Your best choices are stainless steel or bronze as they won't rust.

Whatever kind of pad and cinch you chose, you'll want to clean them regularly. All the things horses come in contact with (dirt, manure, twigs, burrs, etc.) can stick to them and annoy your horse. Sweat and dirt from your horse will also build up on the pad and girth and irritate his skin. Wash them regularly, following the directions that come with the pad/blanket and cinch.

Every time you finish riding, let your pad air dry by hanging it up. Never lay a wet or damp saddle pad or blanket on top of your saddle. Sweat can weaken stitching and darken leather, not to mention make your saddle dirty.

Bridles & Bits

Just as with choosing a saddle, the type of bridle you pick will depend on what events and activities you're doing with your horse. For example, in some classes you can't have a throatlatch on the headstall.

Some Western bridles have a browband, while others just have a loop for one ear to fit through, which is called a "one-ear" headstall. There are also headstalls with two loops, one for each ear, and they are called "two-ear" headstalls.

You'll find many different headstalls to choose from, some flashy and others simple. Headstalls with decorative silver conchos and fancy leatherwork can be quite expensive, but you needn't spend a great deal to have a good bridle.

A one-ear headstall has a loop to go around just one ear.

Your trainer can help you decide which bit is best for your horse. Again, the events you are riding in will help determine these choices, as some classes require that you compete with a particular type of bit. In reining, for example, horses are typically shown in a curb style bit. Curb bits and some snaffles require a curb strap, which goes under the horse's chin and attaches to the bit on both sides of his mouth. Both leather and chain curb straps are available in a variety of styles, so make sure the strap you select is allowed in the event you ride.

When it comes to reins, you'll pick from numerous styles and materials. In many Western events and classes, leather split reins are common. Romal reins are also popular, and consist of round, braided decorative reins that are attached at the end unlike leather split reins, which are two separate reins. Romal reins have a leather "popper" on the end.

In competitions such as barrel racing, pole bending and other speed events, riders use a single-piece rein known as a "sport rein" or "game rein." These reins usually attach to the bit with snaps on each end and are much shorter than standard leather reins. In addition to leather, they may be made of nylon or cotton webbing, or a combination of materials.

Reins come in different lengths and widths, so handle a number of different ones before you buy them to be sure they feel comfortable in your hand. Reins attach to the bit in different ways, and this may also influence your choice.

You'll want to keep your bridle clean. To do this, wipe it down regularly with a soft, dry cloth. At least several times a year you should clean it with saddle soap, a sponge and water, just as you would your saddle. Be sure to remove the bit and unbuckle all the pieces of the bridle so you can clean it thoroughly. Then hang it to dry completely before applying any type of conditioner or oil.

Leg Protection

Depending on what event(s) you participate in, your horse may need leg protectors. It may also be a smart idea to use them when practicing at home or at your trainer's place. Sometimes a horse can bump himself when he's doing certain maneuvers or working fast. Your trainer can help you decide if your horse should have leg protection and what kind is needed.

Boots or polo wraps can help support and protect all four legs. Run-down boots protect the hind legs when a horse is doing hard stops and turns. Bell boots can be used on both front and back feet to help keep the horse from hitting himself on the coronary band or hoof bulb, or from snatching a front shoe off with a hind foot.

It's a good idea to rinse your bit off every time you remove the bridle so it's clean for your horse the next time you ride. It's not pleasant for him if the bit is caked with dried slobber when you put on the bridle.

Run-down boots

Boots offer protection and support.

This horse has both boots and bell boots for protection on his front feet.

3. Halter & Showmanship at Halter

Think you have a beautiful horse? A halter class is a great way to show off your horse's conformation, or build, and get a judge's opinion on how he compares to other horses. Instead of being ridden, horses in a halter class are led by their handler and shown with a leather halter and leather chain-lead shank.

Halter classes can be found at both breed shows – events that are only open to one specific breed – and also at "open" shows, events that allow horses of different breeds to enter. For example, at a Quarter Horse show, only registered Quarter Horses may

be entered. At an open show, classes may include horses from numerous different breeds, and your horse does not have to be registered or purebred to enter.

In a breed show, all the horses are the same breed and the judge evaluates the conformation of each horse in the halter class to see how well he compares to the highest quality of that breed.

At an open show where horses of several different breeds may be in the same halter class, the judge evaluates each horse according to the ideal qualities of that horse's

Horses should stand "square" when asked to line up.

Always leave one horse length in-between horses if you are asked to line up head-to-tail.

specific breed or type. Some shows, for example, have "stock type" halter classes and this is open to horses of stock horse breeding, such as Quarter Horses, Paints, Appaloosas, grade and unregistered. Although there may be horses of different breeds in the same open halter class, the judge is not comparing the horses to each other, as much as comparing them to the ideal of their own breed or type.

Most shows will have different halter classes divided by sex and age. There are usually classes for weanlings, yearlings, two-year-olds, three-year-olds, four-year-olds and older. Classes are also divided by sex of the horse. The larger the show, the more halter classes are offered.

Each exhibitor leads his or her horse into the ring and approaches the judge one at a time. As the horse approaches, the judge steps to the side so the horse can be jogged to a certain point in the ring, usually marked by a cone.

When your horse is walking and jogging, the judge looks at his conformation and also his way of moving. The horse should be balanced and smooth with a good quality way of going.

The horse and handler typically turn left after the cone and then line up along the wall or fence of the ring, or wherever the ring steward tells them to go.

Depending on the class, you may be asked to line up side-by-side or head-to-tail. Always leave one horse length in between if you are required to stand head-to-tail.

During the lineup, the judge inspects each horse individually, looking at the horse from both sides, front and rear. The judge considers how the horse is built and evaluates his characteristics and overall balance.

When the judge inspects your horse, you should always move to stand on the opposite side of the horse. For example, if the judge is on the horse's left side, you should step over and stand on the horse's right. When the judge walks around the horse, you simply step over to stand on the other side. You should look at the judge and make eye contact whenever he or she looks your way.

When standing still, your horse should be "squared up," meaning all four legs are squarely under his body, with his front legs in line together and his back legs in line together. Viewed from either side, the judge should just see two legs (front and back) if the horse is standing perfectly square.

If a horse shows any lameness, that horse is excused from the class and will not be placed. Judges also excuse a horse that has a negative characteristic such as "parrot mouth," in which the horse's top teeth extend farther than the bottom teeth.

At the end of the class, the judge announces the placings, and ribbons are distributed from first through sixth place. To determine the overall Grand Champion Halter Horse and Reserve Champion, judges then evaluate the horses that placed first and second from all halter classes at the show. The Grand Champion and Reserve Champion are chosen from these horses as the two best representatives of their breed or type.

Although the exhibitor is not being judged, your attire should be neat and tidy and complement your horse. The horse should stand out, not the exhibitor. In halter and showmanship classes, many exhibitors wear a Western-style jacket over their shirt with Western polyester dress pants, also called showmanship pants. Western boots and a matching Western hat complete the outfit. Gloves are optional.

Although halter horses are not judged on their attitude, a quiet, easy-going horse will do better in a halter class than a nervous or impatient horse. A judge has the right to excuse any horse that is acting up or showing bad manners.

To compete in a halter class, your horse should:
- Have good conformation
- Know how to lead well
- Stand square and still when you stop
- Be patient and quiet
- Be immaculately clean and well-groomed
- Be fit and in good condition
- Wear a well-fitting, clean leather show halter

Choose your attire so that the colors complement your horse.

Training at Home

Some people think there's not much to a halter class since you aren't riding the horse, but you still have to spend plenty of time working with your horse before you can show him.

You want to make sure the halter fits correctly. The noseband should lie halfway between the horse's nose and eye, and the fit should be snug but not tight.

The chain of the lead shank should go through the left side ring, under the chin, through the ring on the right side and attach to the top right ring. This should leave about

To compete in a halter class you should:
- Have schooled your horse well at home so you are prepared
- Make sure your horse & tack are clean and neat
- Know how to present your horse to the judge properly
- Pay close attention to the ring steward and any instructions given
- Wear proper attire
- Handle your horse with confidence

Make sure your halter fits properly and isn't loose.

four inches of chain coming from the left halter ring, but you want to hold the shank, not the chain, when leading.

Your horse must lead well and his head should be at your right shoulder at all times. He shouldn't be walking out in front of you or dragging behind you. Your right hand should be holding the lead shank near the halter, not the snap or chain part of the lead. The "tail" or excess lead shank should be loosely coiled in your left hand. Never fold or roll the end of the lead shank.

The chain goes through the left side ring, under the chin, through the right side ring, and attaches to the top right ring.

Practice at home until your horse will walk willingly at your side. He should start walking as soon as you walk and stop as soon as you stop.

Hold the leather shank – not the chain – when leading your horse.

Because it's important for your horse to stand square, you will need to teach him this. In the beginning, you will probably need to pick up his feet and put them in place where they should be. Once his feet are in the correct position, tell him to stand and then back up a step. The goal is for your horse to stand still and square without moving his feet until you cue him to walk again.

You don't want to bore your horse when teaching him to stand, so only work on this lesson in short sessions.

Practice stopping and standing. Once he is square, tell him to stand and stay there for a few minutes. Then walk off about ten feet and ask him to stand again. Once he learns, all you will have to do is stop and he will stand still and square.

With most horses, it just takes about a week of training sessions to learn. Once he understands and is doing what you want, don't keep drilling him on it. Just practice enough to keep him fresh.

A halter horse should be fit and not overly fat, so exercise is important. Of course, if you are showing a young horse, such as a weanling or yearling, you don't want to overdo it on exercise. Too much forced exercise can damage young joints and strain muscles.

Showmanship at halter is not just another halter class. It is a different kind of competition in which the skills of the exhibitor are judged instead of the horse's conformation. In these classes, the horse is basically considered a prop to demonstrate the handler's abilities and preparation. Showmanship at halter classes are open to youth and amateur exhibitors, although youth do not compete against adults.

Horses are shown in a leather halter and leather chain lead shank. Depending on the show, exhibitors may enter the ring as a group or one at a time. Each horse and handler must complete the pattern, which is posted by the judge at least one hour before the class. It's up to you to know the pattern and complete it correctly.

You may be asked to walk, jog or do an extended trot, and back up in a straight or curved line. Depending on the pattern, you may have to make partial or full turns or a combination of turns. There are usually

There are usually several cones in the showmanship pattern.

several cones in the pattern to designate points at which to turn. After completing the pattern, you should line up and your horse should stand square for inspection.

Half of the score is based on the overall appearance of the exhibitor and horse, and the other half is based on how well the pattern is performed.

Western attire is worn in the showmanship at halter class unless you are showing English. The judge looks for a clean, neat appearance. Clothes help catch the judge's eye, but you don't want to be gaudy or overdone. You want to make a crisp, tidy impression. You should wear a Western hat, boots, shirt, jacket, and showmanship pants, not jeans.

When choosing your clothing, keep in mind that the colors should complement the color of your horse. For example, if you have a dark bay horse, you wouldn't want to wear black because this would just blend in with the color of the horse. With a dark-colored horse, colors such as red, green, turquoise or blue are appealing. On the other hand, if you have a light-colored horse, such as a gray or palomino, you could wear dark colors and this would complement your horse.

Your hat must match your outfit. If you wear black pants, your hat should be black. If your pants are light or sand-colored, then your hat should be a similar light color. You should never wear spurs or chaps in a showmanship at halter class.

Attitude counts! You should be confident, courteous, professional and sportsmanlike at all times. The pattern should be executed with precision because points will be taken off the score if it's done incorrectly.

When leading the horse from his left side, your right hand should be holding the lead shank near the halter, not on the snap or chain part of the lead. The tail, or excess lead shank, should be loosely coiled in your left hand. Never fold or roll the end of the lead shank. Both arms should be bent at the elbow, but don't look stiff or artificial. You should only lead the horse with one hand.

When making a turn, you should turn your body to the side so that you are facing the horse's head and move him away from you. When you have to back the horse, you should turn from your leading position so that you're facing the rear of the horse. You back the horse by extending your right hand across your chest and walking forward while the horse backs up.

You should never stand in front of the horse when backing him or at any time during the class. You aren't allowed to touch the horse and should control him only with your right hand on the lead shank. Points will be deducted if you kick at or point at your horse's feet to get him to "square up."

Even though the horse is not being judged, the judge will watch how he leads, turns and backs to see how much control the exhibitor has. The horse should not hold his head or neck crooked when turning, leading, stopping or backing up.

To compete in a showmanship at halter class, your horse should:
- Know how to lead well
- Listen and obey your cues to walk, jog, turn, back and stop
- Stand square and still when you stop
- Be immaculately clean and well-groomed
- Be fit and in good condition

To compete in a showmanship at halter class you should:
- Practice at home so you are thoroughly prepared
- Make sure your horse is in good condition, clean and well-groomed
- Be sure your horse's halter fits well and has a clean & neat appearance
- Make sure your attire complements the color of your horse
- Know how to present your horse to the judge properly
- Memorize and complete the pattern correctly
- Handle your horse with confidence & poise
- Never stand directly in front of your horse
- Not touch your horse at any time during the class

Training at Home

Since control of the horse is so important in a showmanship at halter class, you will want to practice at home so you and your horse work smoothly together. Just as in a halter class, you need to teach your horse to lead well and to stand square.

You can set up cones and practice walking toward and around the cones. Practice leading your horse in both straight and curving lines so you will be prepared no matter what the pattern requires.

How you stand when the judge inspects your horse is important and will be considered during the judging. Whenever you present your horse to the judge, you typically stand to left front of your horse facing him on an angle. Your feet should be together and pointed toward the horse's opposite front foot.

In halter and showmanship classes, the "quarter method" is commonly used. To learn where to stand, imagine your horse is divided into four quarters: right front, left front, left rear and right rear.

Because the goal is always to give the judge an unobstructed view of your horse, you change where you stand according to where the judge stands during inspection. For example, when the judge is at your horse's right front quarter, you should be standing in the left front quarter. As the judge moves to the right rear quarter of the horse, you step across the front in three smooth steps, and stand in the horse's right front quarter.

If the judge is at the front of your horse, stand in your horse's left front quarter so you don't obstruct the judge's view.

As the judge moves to the horse's right rear quarter, you should be standing in the horse's right front quarter.

As the judge moves to the horse's left rear quarter, you cross in front of the horse again taking three neat steps, and move back to the horse's left front quarter. When the judge walks up into the left front quarter, you again cross over into the horse's right front quarter and stay there until the judge gives you a direction or moves to the horse's right front.

As the judge moves to the horse's left rear quarter, you should move back to stand in the horse's left front quarter.

Any time you are presenting a horse, whether you are in the front left or front right quarter, you should stand angled towards the front of your horse with your body centered between his eye and muzzle.

Even though the horse's conformation is not judged in this class, the judge will definitely be paying close attention to the horse's appearance and condition. You'll want to make sure your horse is healthy, in good shape, clean and well-groomed. His mane, face, whiskers and the hair on his fetlocks should be neatly trimmed.

As the judge moves to the horse's left front quarter, you again cross over to the horse's right front quarter.

Just spraying a coat conditioner on your horse won't do the trick. If he has a proper nutrition and deworming program, and is groomed regularly, his coat should be in excellent shape.

If your horse has white markings or spots, they must be spic and span. Some exhibitors use baby power or cornstarch to brighten up the horse's white areas.

Hooves should be in excellent condition, whether shod or barefoot. Many exhibitors use hoof polish, which is available in black and clear, to add a nice finishing touch. This is strictly personal preference as hoof polish is not required in a halter or showmanship class.

If you do use polish, make sure the hoof is totally dry and clean before applying it to the outside surface of the hoof only. You'll want to keep your horse standing on a clean, dirt-free surface, such as a rubber mat or concrete floor, until the polish has dried completely.

When presenting your horse, always stand angled toward the front of the horse.

A banded mane makes a neat impression.

In English classes, exhibitors usually braid their horse's mane, tail and forelock, but in a Western halter or showmanship class, your horse's mane should be banded. The mane is evenly divided into small, even sections which are held in place with rubber bands placed close to the base of the mane. Once the mane is banded, the ends are evenly trimmed so the mane is no less than three inches long.

Banding the mane presents a very neat picture to the judge. It can also improve the look of your horse. For example, if your horse has a short, thick neck, banding the mane will actually make his neck appear longer and sleeker.

You can learn how to band a mane by practicing and watching someone who is experienced. In the beginning, it's best to have someone knowledgeable do the task so you know it's done correctly. Your trainer can help you locate a good person to band your horse's mane.

4. Western Pleasure

One of the most popular Western classes at horse shows today is Western pleasure. Just as the name implies, this class highlights horses that are a pleasure to ride under Western tack.

All exhibitors in the class compete at the same time, riding around the perimeter of the arena as they follow the judge's commands to walk, jog (trot), lope (canter), and reverse directions. The horses will also be asked to stop, stand quietly and back up on cue. At some shows, the judge will ask for an extended trot and even a hand gallop.

Judges are looking for a pretty-moving horse that has balanced, forward motion. Each gait should be even, rhythmic, and ground covering. Short-striding, choppy horses will not do well in this class! A horse that responds quietly and easily to his rider and has smooth, flowing gaits has a much better chance of placing in the ribbons than a horse that is rough, ill-tempered, or hard to control.

Judges don't want to see a horse going excessively slow or overly fast. Incorrect head position, breaking gait, or picking up the wrong lead will also make a horse lose points with the judge.

Western pleasure horses should look happy and relaxed as they travel on a loose rein.

Horses are judged on their attitude and movement, and shouldn't travel too slowly or too quickly.

The judge wants to see a happy and relaxed horse carrying his head and neck fairly level with, or just slightly above, his withers. His head and neck should be neither too low nor too high. Your horse should carry his head in a normal collected manner so that his head is straight up and down when viewed from the side. He shouldn't be "behind the vertical," with his nose tucked in towards his chest, and he shouldn't be "in front of the vertical," with his nose poked out.

Each horse is judged on his quality of movement, attitude and how well he travels on a loose rein. Even though the rider is not judged in this class, horse and rider must work as a team and the whole picture they present together must be appealing. In the Western pleasure class, your goal as a rider is to sell your horse to the judge and give him a reason to place you.

> Horses are placed according to the judge's opinion, not scored for performing specific tasks. If the class is at a breed show, judges follow the rule book for that specific breed.

Western pleasure riders typically ride with a fairly long stirrup so they sit deep in the saddle. Even though you're not being judged, it's important to have proper position in the saddle so you have good control of your horse and help him remain balanced.

At most breed shows, a "junior horse" is five years of age or younger and can be

Riding with a fairly long stirrup helps the rider sit deep in the saddle.

class. You may ride with either your right or left hand, but whichever hand is not on the reins must rest at your side and never touch the horse, saddle, or any part of your body while competing.

When riding with one hand, your horse must know how to "neck rein," as described in Chapter 1. The reins should be held between your pointer and middle fingers, and your thumb should be on top, never on the bottom or with your hand held flat. As you are riding and guiding your horse, your rein hand should always remain in the middle of your horse's neck, just in front of the saddle horn. There should be enough slack that the rein is loose when you put your hand down, but when you pick up the reins you should have light contact with the horse's mouth.

shown in a snaffle, bosal hackamore, or curb bit. A "senior horse" is six or older and must be shown in a "full bridle," which means a bit with shanks that operates off leverage. Examples of such bits are a curb or a Tom Thumb snaffle. Be sure to check the rule book because some bits are considered illegal. If you are caught showing in such a bit, you can be disqualified.

If you are showing a young horse and riding with a snaffle bit, you ride with two hands on the reins. In any other type bit, you must only use one hand in the Western pleasure

You can hold the reins with either your left or right hand, but your free hand must never touch the horse, saddle or your body.

Hold the reins between your pointer and middle fingers.

The secret is to be able to guide your horse with cues that are so subtle they aren't obvious to anyone watching, and that includes the judge. Always use your leg cue first to guide your horse to turn, instead of using your hand first.

Any time you're showing in a class with other exhibitors, there is a chance for your horse to get cut off, or for a horse in front of you to slow down or even stop unexpectedly. You don't want to get caught in traffic in the show ring because your goal is always to make a good impression on the judge.

You can avoid traffic problems by constantly watching the other horses in front of and behind you. Since you want to show your horse to the best of his ability, you want the judge to be able to see you each time around the ring. If a horse in front of you is going so slowly that your horse might have to break gait, go off the rail just to pass that horse and then get back on the rail. Don't go inside the slow horse along the rail because then you are hidden from the judge for a time.

Appearance Counts

While the rider's equitation is not judged in a Western pleasure class, you must be comfortably in control of your horse at all times. Rider attire is also important and the outfit you chose can make your horse stand out either positively or negatively.

Riders must wear long-sleeved shirts, jeans or Western-style dress pants, and chaps.

Chose your outfit carefully so you make an overall attractive picture.

Some female riders wear glittery show shirts and fancy jewelry, but this isn't necessary to win. Boots and Western hat should be the same color, and your shirt and pants should coordinate with your horse's saddle pad color. For example, if you wear a solid-colored shirt, your horse's saddle pad can be multi-colored, but if you decide to wear a patterned shirt, then the saddle pad should be solid.

Remember, you're trying to create that pretty overall picture, so you don't want to have clashing patterns or have your outfit appear too busy. (Look back at the chapter on halter and showmanship for tips on choosing the best color to show off your horse, depending on his coat color.)

Your horse must be shown in Western tack, including a Western saddle and a bridle without a noseband. The style of headstall you choose can affect the appearance of your horse's head. For example, a two-ear headstall can improve the look of a horse with a long head and longish ears, while a headstall with a browband can actually make a horse's head appear wider than it is.

A light-oil colored saddle is preferred for Western pleasure, along with a matching headstall and reins. Reins must be "split" (two separate reins), and you can't have a knot, buckle, or "keeper" to hold the reins together. While you don't have to buy a saddle and bridle that are loaded with silver, a bit of silver will help catch the judge's eye and show off your horse.

Of course, you want your horse to be clean and immaculately groomed with his legs, ears, muzzle and bridle path neatly clipped. Western pleasure horses are known for their long, flowing tails, no matter what the breed. Some breeds are even shown with tail extensions or artificial tails if their natural tail is short or sparse.

Length of the bridle path will vary according to breed, with stock horse breeds typically having a shorter bridle path than Arabians, Morgans and gaited breeds.

A light-oil colored saddle and matching headstall are preferred for Western pleasure.

Breed will also determine how your horse's mane should be presented in the class. Stock horse types are usually shown with "banded" manes to make the manes lie flat and create a tidy appearance. Other breeds are shown with long, loose, unbanded manes. Braided forelocks are common in many breeds.

Conchos give a flashy look to a bridle.

Silver conchos and decorations add style to a show saddle.

History of Conchos

Western saddles and bridles often have silver conchos as decorations. The word actually comes from "concha," the Spanish word for "seashell."

The Native American Indians of the Great Plains and Mexican vaqueros were the first to decorate their tack with conchos. Great Plains Indians also used the silver pieces as hair ornaments and decorations. Navajo Indians adopted the conchos to use on belts and created a strong tradition of unique concho belts that is still highly valued today.

The earliest conchos were likely made of silver dollars that were hammered flat, and then stamped with designs and edged in varying patterns.

Usually round or oval, conchos are sometimes rectangular, and can be made of nickel, silver plate or sterling silver. They attach to saddles and bridles by a screw back that makes it easy to replace or add conchos.

Training at Home

Because the competition can be tough in Western pleasure classes, you'll want to practice so that you and your horse are totally ready before entering a show. There are many instructors who work with students competing in Western pleasure, and you may want to find a trainer who specializes in this area.

You should be able to walk, jog and lope your horse in both directions by giving very subtle cues. This takes practice. You never want your horse to be in a hurry, so you will have to spend plenty of time working with him so that he waits for your cues. The goal is to have a horse that is willing, relaxed and never hurrying, but still has good forward movement.

Work on perfecting your jog so the horse is smooth, steady and very responsive at this gait before you work on developing the same at the lope.

The judge will mark off if a horse is on the incorrect lead, so you always want to pick up the correct lead at the lope so that the horse's inside legs (away from the rail)

Get to the show grounds early enough that you have plenty of time to prepare your horse for your first class without rushing.

extend the furthest. Your cue leg to ask for the lope should be given with your "outside" leg, the leg closest to the rail. Practice picking up both the left and right lead as you travel in both directions.

Practice turning in one direction at a walk and then pick up the lope as you come out of the turn. Do this in both directions so you can work on both leads. Once your horse always takes the correct lead coming out of a turn, you can practice picking up different leads at the lope while traveling straight. Your horse should keep his head level, even when going into the lope.

Transitions between gaits are important so practice going smoothly from a walk to a jog (slightly faster than a walk), or trot, and from a walk to a lope. You also want to have smooth downward transitions from a jog to a walk and from a lope to a jog and walk.

Practice backing up in a straight line. Your horse shouldn't raise or toss his head when you ask him to back. You shouldn't pull back on the reins to ask your horse to back. Instead, maintain light contact with his mouth on the reins so he knows not to walk forward, and at the same time squeeze with your legs. Release the pressure of your legs as soon as he starts to back up so he knows that he's doing the right thing. Remember, squeeze and release is much more effective than constant pressure.

As you practice at home, notice if your horse tries to drift to the inside away from the rail. If he does, you need to use your inside leg (the one closest to the inside of the arena) to block and keep him from drifting.

Believe it or not, your horse always tends to go in the direction you are looking, so maintain your focus up and straight ahead.

You want the horse to keep his head level when moving into a lope.

Don't look down at the ground or at your horse. If you look to the inside of the arena, your horse will start drifting in that same direction.

Add Variety!

If you do the same thing every time you ride, you and your horse will both get bored. Even though you want to do well at Western pleasure, you should do more than just ride around the rail of the arena when practicing. If this is all you do, your horse will start to dread riding. You can get in good sessions by practicing different gaits on the trail and out of the arena. When you do ride in the arena, don't just stay on the rail; use the entire arena to liven things up.

Pay attention to your horse's actions. If you notice your horse swishing his tail, he may be resisting because he's bored or frustrated, or you may be asking him to do something he doesn't understand. He could also just be tired of repetitive training.

Head tossing is a sign your horse may be resisting your hands, or it could be that he is nervous or uncomfortable with the bit you are using. Tail swishing and head tossing can also be signs of discomfort. For example, the saddle may not fit correctly or a piece of tack may not be adjusted properly.

Since our horses can't talk, they use body language to communicate and it's up to us as their caretakers and riders to stop and investigate what they're trying to tell us.

It takes practice to get competitive at this class, but never forget the reason you started riding in the first place, and that is to have fun! Vary your training routines to keep things interesting. Keep in mind the "pleasure" part of Western pleasure and try to practice in ways that are interesting for your horse.

5. Western Horsemanship

If you want to prove your ability at handling your horse, the Western horsemanship class is an excellent goal. In this class, the rider – not the horse – is judged on his or her horsemanship ability. These classes are open to youth and amateur riders.

Western horsemanship is a pattern class in which each exhibitor competes individually and performs a prescribed pattern that includes maneuvers performed at a walk, trot, and lope. Some patterns may require an extended trot or extended lope. Maneuvers include straight lines, curved lines, serpentines, circle or figure-eight, turn or pivot, stop, back up, rollback on the haunches or on the forehand, sidepass, two-track or leg yield, flying change or simple lead change, and counter canter. Exhibitors are sometimes asked to ride without stirrups for a portion of the pattern.

The judge may ask you to ride without stirrups for part of the class, so practice this at home to be prepared.

> Depending on the show and the judge's preference, you may be asked to walk into the ring one at a time and perform your pattern, or you may enter as a group and then perform the pattern one at a time as the judge calls you out.

After every rider in the class has performed the pattern, the judge may ask the entire group, or just the finalists, to ride the rail, depending on the judge's preference. Exhibitors are asked to walk, trot and lope at least one direction of the area. This gives the judge another look at each rider and also reveals how each rider controls his or her horse in a group.

In Western horsemanship, riders are judged on body position, their seat in the saddle and how well they control their horse. An exhibitor who maintains proper position while performing all maneuvers will score higher than a rider who doesn't maintain position.

Judging is based on a score of zero to 20, with 20 being the highest score possible for excellence. Ten points are given for the overall presentation of horse and rider, and 10 points for performance during the class. Among the faults that count against a rider are sloppy, dirty or poor-fitting attire, a hat coming off during the class, obvious cues with legs or hand on reins, a horse in dirty or poor condition, ill-fitting equipment, staring at the judge or holding your head in a crooked, unnatural or stiff body position, toes down in the stirrup, holding arms straight instead of bent at the elbow, looking at the ground while riding, etc.

The judge also marks off for taking the wrong lead, a crooked back up, a horse showing resistance to the rider's cues, a horse's head carried too high or too low, an over-flexed neck, a nose carried out, rough transitions, a horse's head carried crooked, hesitation during maneuvers, etc.

A horse and rider may be disqualified for going off pattern or knocking over a cone in the pattern.

If you have proper body position, you'll be better able to control your horse.

In horsemanship classes, you will have a specified number of strides or a specific location to change leads. The judge will be watching to see that lead changes are timely and executed smoothly.

The cues you give your horse should be subtle and not obvious to the judge. Showmanship and attitude are important in the Western horsemanship class because the judge will be watching each rider closely.

While the horse isn't being judged, how well he performs – or doesn't perform – relates directly to the rider's ability. If the rider can't control the horse and complete the pattern correctly, that rider won't score well, no matter how beautiful or well turned-out the horse may be.

For example, a pattern may require that you back your horse a certain number of steps. Although the horse isn't being judged, if he can't perform the maneuver and back the correct number of steps in a smooth, straight line, this will affect your score since the judge is looking to see how well you can control and maneuver your horse. He wants to see how well the horse and rider work together as a team.

The pattern for each class must be posted at least one hour before the class begins. It's up to you as the exhibitor to memorize the pattern and complete it correctly. Not only will the judge be looking to see if the pattern is done properly, but he wants to see that each maneuver is performed with precision and smoothness. At the same time, the rider should be balanced and maintaining correct body position in the saddle.

Just as in Western pleasure, your horse's head and neck should be neither too low nor too high. He should carry his head and neck fairly level with, or just slightly above, his withers, and his head should be in a normal collected manner so that when viewed from the side his head is straight up and down. He shouldn't be behind the vertical, with his nose tucked in toward his chest, and he shouldn't be in front of the vertical, with his nose poked out.

The judge wants to see your horse carry his head and neck straight when traveling in a straight line and slightly arched to the inside when traveling in a circle or on a curve.

In the Western horsemanship class, you may ride with only one hand on the reins unless you are showing a young horse in a snaffle, in which case you may ride with two hands on the reins. In either case, your hand(s) holding the reins should be just above or slightly in front of the saddle horn.

Hold the reins just above or slightly in front of the saddle horn, and be sure to maintain light contact with the horse's mouth.

You should maintain light contact with the horse's mouth so that only slight hand movements are necessary to cue the horse. The judge will penalize a rider whose reins are too loose or too tight.

When riding with one hand, you may use either your left or right, but you can't switch hands during the class. Your free hand and arm can either be carried bent at the elbow like the hand holding the reins, or it may be carried straight at the rider's side. At no time should the free hand touch your body, the reins or the horse, and you should never hold onto the saddle horn or any part of the saddle. Illegal use of the hands on the reins during a class can result in disqualification.

Just as in Western pleasure, rider attire is important and should show you and your horse in a positive manner. Riders must wear long-sleeved shirts, jeans or Western-

Many riders carry their free arm bent at the elbow with the empty hand next to the hand holding the reins.

Make sure your free hand never touches your body, the reins or your horse.

style dress pants, and chaps. Boots and Western hat should be the same color, and your shirt and pants should coordinate with your horse's saddle pad color. Don't pick an outfit that clashes with your horse's color or is too busy.

Your horse must be shown in Western tack, including a Western saddle and a bridle without a noseband. A light-oil colored saddle is preferred, along with a matching headstall and reins. You must use split reins without a knot, buckle or "keeper" to hold the reins together.

Overall appearance is important and that means your horse and all equipment should be immaculately clean and in good condition.

To compete in a Western horsemanship class, your horse should:
- Be attentive, well trained and responsive to your cues
- Travel at an even, smooth speed in each gait – not too fast or too slow
- Back up straight and smoothly on cue
- Carry his head in a natural collected position with his head and neck level with or slightly above his withers
- Pick up the correct leads
- Make smooth transitions between gaits
- Be able to perform all required maneuvers smoothly and with precision
- Carry his head and neck straight when traveling in a straight line and slightly arched to the inside when traveling in a circle or on a curve

To compete in a Western horsemanship class you should:
- Appear poised and confident at all times
- Maintain proper position in the saddle at all gaits and when performing maneuvers
- Feel very comfortable riding and controlling your horse at all gaits
- Always look in the direction your horse is traveling, never down or off to the side
- Be able to control and cue your horse with light contact on the reins
- Understand all required maneuvers and know how to cue your horse to perform them
- Wear attire that coordinates with your horse's color and saddle pad
- Present a neat overall picture

Training at Home

Working with a trainer who is familiar with Western horsemanship will be a great help as you practice for this class. You and your horse should know how to ride smoothly and comfortably at all three gaits and you also need to know how to perform a variety of different maneuvers because you won't know until the show just what maneuvers your pattern will require.

> Just as with Western pleasure, it's important to have smoothness and even cadence in all gaits. Your horse should never appear to be in a hurry, but he shouldn't be slow and pokey either.

The judge will be looking for good equitation, so you must maintain correct body position in the saddle at all times. You can't practice this enough! Always strive to be in the proper position whether you are riding in the arena or just out on the trail riding with friends.

A lot of the training you will need to do for Western horsemanship will involve practicing the different maneuvers. Because there will be cones used in some parts of the pattern, you should use cones when practicing at home so your horse is familiar with them. Your cues shouldn't be obvious to anyone watching and this takes practice. For example, if you have to sidepass, your hands should be still and your leg cues to your horse should be very subtle.

The judge doesn't want to notice you asking your horse to do something; he just wants to see the end result, which is the horse quietly and smoothly executing the maneuvers. The goal is for you and your horse to present a harmonious picture together. Making this a reality requires spending many hours training and working with your horse so that you function as a team.

Here are some of the maneuvers you should practice:

Circles – Work to keep your circles round and at a consistent speed, whatever gait you are riding.

Stopping – Your main cues to stop should come from your seat, not your hands. When you stop, both you and your horse should be square and stop smoothly. Your shoulders should always be in line with your horse's shoulders.

Back up – Practice backing so that your horse backs smoothly and in a straight line. He should be responsive and never hold his head high or turned to avoid your cues.

Turns – Make your turns smooth and continuous without hesitation or backing up of any kind. When turning on the haunches, you want the horse to plant his inside hind leg and pivot around as he steps across with his front legs while keeping that hind foot in the same place.

Rollback – Practice stopping and then rolling back 180 degrees as your horse turns back over his hocks. He shouldn't hesitate in the rollback or back up.

Sidepass – Even though your horse is moving to the side, his body should be straight, not curving at all. He should step across with both his front and hind legs as he moves laterally (sideways). He shouldn't move forward at all, just to the side.

Leg Yield – The horse should continue moving forward and also laterally (sideways) when you ask him to leg yield. His body should be in a slight arc opposite of the direction that he is moving. For example, if you are leg yielding to the left, the horse is moving off your right leg and his body should be arced slightly to the right while he moves forward and laterally to the left. His front and hind legs should both step across.

Two-Track – At the two-track, your horse should step across with both his front and hind legs while moving forward and laterally in a diagonal direction. His body should be slightly bent opposite the direction he is moving. For example, if you are riding to the left, his body should have a slight bend

Keep your circles consistent and perfectly round.

Your turns should be smooth without any hesitation.

Rollback: In the rollback, your horse turns back over his hocks 180 degrees.

to the right, even though he's traveling to the left.

Counter Canter – If the class calls for a counter canter, your horse must pick up the outside (counter) lead, instead of the inside lead, as is common. You will want to practice the counter canter so you know your horse will perform it when asked. Many horses will automatically try to switch back to loping on the inside lead because they feel more balanced this way, and also because it's a habit.

Practice lead changes so your horse responds promptly when you cue him.

Lead changes – Your horse should know how to pick up his left or right lead whenever you ask. He should be able to do this in response to your leg and seat cues without you having to turn his head. Remember, make sure he is positioned to pick up the correct lead on the hind end and then he will get it right on the front end. You should have lead changes down solid before you advance to flying lead changes, which is when you switch leads without breaking gait at the lope.

Once your horse has learned the basics of a maneuver, you can practice while riding down the trail or in a field outside the arena. It's actually more of a challenge to perform the maneuvers in different environments because your horse must be focused only on you. This also keeps your training sessions from becoming repetitious and dull.

With so many maneuvers to learn, you might be thinking that is all you'll have time to do. Wrong! Always remember that practicing doesn't necessarily mean riding around and around an arena working on maneuvers.

6. Trail Class

If you admire a calm, sure-footed horse that can handle many different challenges, the trail class is probably just your style. This class tests the maneuverability of the horse through a series of obstacles, some of which can be quite unusual.

The class is judged according to how well the horse negotiates the various obstacles. The judge looks to see the horse's ability and manners, and how well he responds to his rider. Horses should be willing, attentive, and not delay unnecessarily while going through the course.

Obviously, the goal is for the horse to negotiate each obstacle without making a mistake, but the judge also hopes to see style and attentiveness. For example, let's say there are two horses in the same class who make no mistakes. The first horse is hesitant or reluctant over some obstacles

The judge wants to see an attentive, alert horse that shows courage and interest in each obstacle.

and does not appear interested, while the second horse, ears alert, appears engaged and is good at picking his way through the obstacles. The judge is going to score the second horse higher than the first.

A score of 70 is average. Each obstacle has a score that will add or subtract in one-half point increments from the base score of 70, depending on how well the horse performs. Every obstacle has a value of plus 1-1/2 (excellent) to minus 1-1/2 (very poor). For example, ticking a cone, pole, or any part of the obstacle with the hoof is a one-half point deduction, while stepping on the cone, pole, etc. is a full point deduction.

Breaking gait for more than two strides is a three point penalty. Letting go of the gate, a horse refusing an obstacle, dropping an object you must carry, etc., are all five point penalties.

Horse and rider can be disqualified if they perform an obstacle out of order or enter/exit an obstacle from the wrong direction.

The trail course is usually designed so that the horse must walk, trot and lope at some point between obstacles, and the judge will pay attention to the cadence and quality of each gait. This means your horse must be a good riding horse, not just talented at obstacles. When traveling between obstacles, the horse should carry his head and neck in a natural manner and his poll should be level with or slightly above the withers. No matter what gait he is in, his headset should not be too collected or too "nosed out."

While trail classes may vary considerably from show to show, there are always at least six obstacles, including three mandatory obstacles.

Opening, passing through and closing a gate from horseback is a standard trail obstacle. You must keep your hand on the gate at all times while negotiating this challenge.

Riding over four logs or poles is another mandatory obstacle. The logs/poles may be in a straight line or they may be curved, raised or in a zigzag pattern. Depending on the class, the judge may require that the horse walk, trot or lope over the logs/poles.

A backing obstacle is also mandatory and includes backing through and around at least three markers or cones. Or the course may include an obstacle where the horse must back through poles or logs in an "L," "V," "U," or similar shape.

The rider must keep a hand on the gate at all times while opening, going through and closing it.

When riding over poles or logs, your horse should not step on or touch them.

After these mandatory obstacles, the trail course may include many different challenges. You may have to cross a water hazard, such as a ditch or small pond; remove and replace items in a mailbox; carry an object (such as a slicker or bucket) from one part of the ring to another; ride over a wooden bridge; sidepass over a pole or rail; and/or enter a square box of logs or rails and execute a turn inside. Some classes even require the horse to stand ground-tied or hobbled after the rider dismounts and walks a certain distance away.

It's really up to the course designer to create an inventive and challenging course, and some of them get very creative. The course will be posted at least one hour before the class begins, and each exhibitor must memorize it.

Horses are usually ridden in a Western show saddle with a matching color headstall that may be one-ear, two-ear, or have a browband. The exhibitor may use an approved Western bit, such as a curb or shank bit, and ride with one hand. If using a snaffle bit or

Because each horse competes one at a time, it can sometimes take hours for final results to be announced, depending on the size of the trail class.

Backing through an "L" or other shaped obstacle requires that your horse respond closely to your cues.

a bosal hackamore, the rider can use two hands.

The rider's attire is basically the same as in a Western pleasure class, as described in Chapter 4.

A wooden bridge is a common trail class obstacle.

To compete in a trail class, your horse should:
- Be attentive, well trained and responsive to your cues
- Know how to negotiate a wide variety of obstacles since you won't know until the show what the course will include
- Travel smoothly and evenly at the walk, trot, and lope without breaking gait
- Know how to pick up lead departures in both directions
- Know how to back up smoothly in a straight line
- Know how to sidepass over a pole or log
- Carry his head in a natural collected position with his head and neck level with or slightly above his withers
- Not balk, refuse or show hesitation while negotiating obstacles
- Know how to stand quietly ground-tied while you walk away

To compete in a trail class you should:
- Feel very comfortable riding and controlling your horse at all gaits
- Memorize the course so you approach each obstacle correctly and in the right sequence
- Appear poised and confident at all times
- Practice a wide variety of obstacles since you cannot be sure exactly what the course will include
- Be comfortable mounting and dismounting in case you have to dismount to hobble or ground-tie your horse during the class
- Be able to put on and remove a slicker while mounted and when standing next to your horse
- Be able to carry an object, such as a bucket with water in it, while riding and then set it down at a designated spot while still mounted
- Remove and place items in a mailbox while mounted

Training at Home

If you're interested in entering trail classes, there are plenty of ways you can practice to improve your skills. Obviously, your horse needs to be well trained and attentive to your cues.

Before you start practicing with various obstacles, your horse must be comfortable performing at all three gaits. You should expect to walk, jog and lope in every trail class, so you'll need to be prepared. A trail class may also require lead departures in both directions, so your horse should pick up the correct lead upon command.

Once you have the basics in place, you will want to be sure your horse knows how to back up, sidepass, yield to your leg in both directions, and step over poles on the ground.

Today's trail classes are much tougher than they were years ago. You and your horse need to be a good team to be successful.

Opening, passing through and closing a gate on horseback is a standard obstacle in every trail class. This takes practice and patience since you must keep your hand on the gate the entire time. This obstacle requires that your horse be able to sidepass, turn and stand close to the gate.

Use a sturdy gate to practice at home and remember to keep one hand on the gate at all times, as your score will be lowered if you don't do this in the show ring.

Practice opening the gate from both sides. For example, if you approach so the gate is on your right, your horse's head should be toward the opening end of the gate, not the hinge end.

Use your left leg to cue your horse to move his hindquarters to the right so he's standing next to the gate. Open the gate, keeping your right hand on the gate. Again use your leg to direct your horse's hindquarters so he moves around and through the gate opening.

At this point, his head should be pointing toward the hinge side of the gate. Now use your leg cues to direct your horse to side-pass right so you can close the gate. Do just the opposite if you approach the gate from your left.

Since negotiating logs/poles is a mandatory part of every trail class, you will want to practice this using four poles that are five to seven feet long. Depending on the course, you may have to walk, trot, or lope over poles, so you will need to set up a variety of pole configurations when practicing.

For walk-overs, poles should be spaced 20 to 24 inches apart. They may also be elevated up to 12 inches high and if elevated, poles must be at least 22 inches apart.

For trot-overs, poles should be spaced three feet to three feet six inches apart. They may be elevated up to eight inches high.

For lope-overs, poles should be spaced six to seven feet apart. They may be elevated up to eight inches off the ground.

Backing through and around markers is another mandatory element in trail classes, so you'll need three cones or similar markers for practice. Set them up in several different patterns so you are prepared because you won't know until you get to the show just what the course looks like.

Keep in mind that course designers can position the poles in either straight, curved or zigzag lines, so you will want to set up poles in different configurations and practice all of these at home.

Weaving between cones while backing up requires precision; you don't want to hit or step on any of the cones.

The three cones may be in a straight line 36 to 40 inches apart and your horse will have to weave between them in a serpentine pattern while backing up without touching or stepping on any cones.

Another backing pattern is to have the cones set up in a triangular pattern about 28 to 36 inches apart. The horse must back between two cones while going around the center cone. This pattern may also be used with logs or rails set in an "L" shape to add more challenge while backing.

Many courses will require that you sidepass over a log or rail. In some cases, the rail may be elevated up to 12 inches, so be sure to practice with a pole on the ground and also elevated.

Here's another instance where the sidepass you and your horse have learned will be put to use. Your horse should freely move sideways in either direction off your leg and seat cues. If you are sidepassing to the left, for instance, hold your hands steady so the horse doesn't try to walk forward. Then press with your right leg and use the right side of your seat muscles to push your horse sideways. If you're sidepassing to the right, do just the opposite.

Take your time when introducing a pole or rail to sidepass over. Always practice sidepassing over a pole flat on the ground and master this before asking your horse to sidepass over an elevated pole.

Your horse should be able to sidepass both directions over a log or pole.

Practice sidepassing over an elevated pole so you are prepared if the course includes this kind of obstacle.

Put your cones six feet apart to practice weaving between them.

Some courses will have an obstacle where where your horse weaves through the cones or markers at a walk or trot in a winding serpentine pattern. When practicing, place the cones/markers a minimum of six feet apart.

A wooden bridge is often part of the trail course. Practicing on a bridge is important so that your horse gets accustomed to the sound and feel of stepping up and walking on this wooden object.

Dismount and lead your horse over the bridge the first few times to get familiar with it. Let him drop his head to sniff and investigate it in the beginning.

Be sure to approach the bridge straight on and don't let your horse step on or off the sides.

In competition, the bridge is usually about six feet long and about three feet wide, so you will want to practice on a bridge that is similar to what you'll encounter at the show.

It doesn't have to be fancy, but it's very important that it be solid and sturdy. If your horse gets frightened of the practice bridge because it's wobbly or unsteady, he will lose confidence and this will be obvious when you are showing.

Riding into an eight foot-square obstacle and executing a turn before exiting is common in trail classes. To make this obstacle at home, you should have four logs or rails that are five to seven feet long. Place them on the ground in a square in your practice area.

Ride into the box and cue the horse to make a complete 360-degree turnaround without touching or stepping on the poles. He must keep all four feet inside the box the entire time he is turning.

Some trail classes will only require a 180-degree turn inside the box, but at home you should practice both full and partial turnarounds so you are prepared once you get to the show.

You may have to ride into an eight foot-square box, execute a complete turn, and then exit. Your horse should turn smoothly without hesitation and not step on any of the poles.

A water obstacle is often used in the trail class and any good trail horse should be able to cross water without a problem. You can start by walking your horse through mud puddles and then gradually move on to riding through larger areas of water.

Some trail courses require exhibitors to open and close a mailbox and put an item in it. You should practice this at home using a sturdy mailbox in a safe place. Don't practice on your family mailbox out along a busy road!

Get your horse used to a slicker when you are standing next to him. Practice putting it on and off until your horse is calm and not bothered by this.

Remember that it takes many small lessons for your horse to learn new obstacles. Take your time and praise him when he makes an effort to do the right thing. Don't bombard him with too many new things at once, and never rush or force him.

Always end your schooling session on a good note by doing something the horse already understands. Let's say you are introducing the bridge to him one day. After you do this, don't end the practice time there. Get on him and do something he is already good at, such as backing up or sidepassing. Then praise him for a job well done and let him relax for a few minutes before you untack and quit for the day.

While you will want to set up a course to practice at home, all your schooling doesn't have to take place in an arena. You may encounter some obstacles on a real trail ride that will help prepare your horse for the trail class. For safety's safe, before you negotiate any natural obstacle you find out on the trail, look at it closely from all sides. Make sure the footing is good and there are no sharp branches or anything else that could hurt you or your horse.

Just because your horse is able to do something - sidepassing over a log, for example - that doesn't mean he would choose to do this on his own out in the pasture. Be a thoughtful partner to your horse and don't ask him to do anything where he could get hurt.

7. Speed Events:
Barrel Racing & Pole Bending

If you love riding fast and enjoy challenging competition, then Western speed events may be just what you're looking for. These events are timed contests in which horse and rider race against the clock for the fastest time. Two of the most popular Western speed events are barrel racing and pole bending.

Horses of any breed may compete in these timed events, but the Quarter Horse and the Appendix Quarter Horse – a Quarter Horse crossed with a Thoroughbred – dominate the sports because of their speed, heart and agility. More important than bloodlines are the talent and willingness of the individual horse. He has to be athletic, intelligent, sound and willing.

Riders must fine-tune their horsemanship skills so they can guide their horses through the patterns at a fast pace.

Barrel racing is a highly popular girls' Western riding sport.

Barrel Racing

Barrel racing competition first started in Texas in the United States. The Women's Professional Rodeo Association (WPRA) began in 1948 and was first known as the Girls Rodeo Association. Although women were allowed to compete in several different rodeo events, barrel racing remains the most popular.

There are several different organizations that govern barrel racing. Women must be at least 18 years old to join the WPRA, but a Junior Division for girls ages 17 and under was recently instituted.

While barrel racing is typically thought of as a sport for women, it is also open to male riders, who compete in National Barrel Horse Association (NBHA) events. The NBHA is the world's largest barrel racing association and features over 250 competition districts throughout the United States, Canada, France, Italy and Panama. Because of the format of competition, any barrel racer, from beginner to expert, can compete and win in NBHA events.

Here is an example of a Barrel Racing Pattern.

In this exciting sport, a triangular course consisting of three 55-gallon drums or heavy plastic barrels is set up in the arena. The distance from each barrel is measured exactly.

These are typically the standard distances between barrels:
- 90 feet between barrel one and two
- 105 feet between barrel one and three and between barrels two and three.
- 60 feet from barrels one and two to score line
- No less than 15 feet from each of the first two barrels and the arena fence
- No less than 25 to 30 feet from the third barrel and the back fence

The horse and rider run the barrels in a "cloverleaf" pattern. They enter the arena at top speed and can start with either the right or left barrel. The horse must circle the first barrel from the inside – the side farthest from the arena fence – so that his path makes a complete circle around it. After

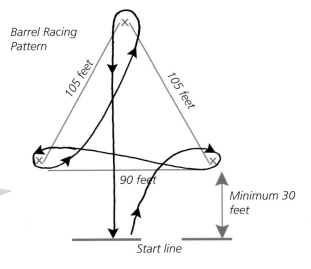

Barrel Racing Pattern

105 feet   105 feet

90 feet

Minimum 30 feet

Start line

completing the first turn, horse and rider race to the second barrel and circle it in the opposite direction. Once they complete this turn, they race on to circle the third and final barrel and circle it in the same direction as the second barrel was taken. Then it's an all-out sprint down the center of the arena until the horse crosses the finish line and the timer stops.

The goal is to have the fastest time but not knock over any barrels. There is a five second penalty added to the time for every barrel knocked over. There is no penalty for bumping or knocking a barrel, so long as it stays upright and doesn't fall over.

An electronic timer or stopwatch is used to time events down to the hundredth of a second. Time begins the instant horse and rider cross over the start line and ends the moment they pass the finish line. The winner is often determined by mere fractions of a second. Times will vary depending on the size of the arena, the talent of the competition and how hard or soft the footing is. A winning time may be anywhere from 12 seconds to 19 seconds, depending on the arena size.

Riders aren't judged on how well they ride or their appearance. It's all about speed, and the fastest time wins.

Just like many other timed sporting events, the start is crucial to a successful run in barrel racing. The rider wants to go as quickly as possible but must rate her horse's speed in the approach to that first barrel. If the horse is going too fast or is not under control, he may run past the barrel and get off the pattern. If this happens, the horse and rider are disqualified and receive a score of "no time."

The area around a barrel is known as the "pocket" and as the horse turns, he should

After turning at the third and final barrel, it's a full-out run for the finish.

stay in this pocket as close to the barrel as possible without hitting it. Although the horse is doing most of the hard work, it's the rider's responsibility to help him by remaining balanced and in correct position.

The rider wants her horse to stay in the pocket close to the barrel while turning.

When the horse digs down for that tight turn around each barrel, the rider should be sitting deep in the saddle and not lean to either side. One hand is holding the reins to guide the horse, while the other hand is braced on the pommel so the rider remains steady in the saddle. The rider should have her legs close to the horse's sides. Sometimes a horse clears the barrel, but is close enough that the rider's leg touches it. For this reason, barrel racers often wear protective leg gear. Horses should also wear leg protection.

The rider should be sitting deep in the saddle as the horse powers around the barrel.

Barrel saddles are lighter weight and smaller than a standard Western stock saddle. The seat is designed in a way that helps the rider sit deep and snugly in the saddle, which is important for those fast, sharp turns.

The saddle pad is shaped in a similar style so that there is not a lot of extra pad extending beyond the saddle. Although any regular Western bridle can be used, the reins will be shorter than usual and consist of one single rein – not two – so there is no chance of dropping them during the run. Many riders also have "stampede strings" on their Western hats to keep them from blowing off.

Barrel saddles are built to help the rider maintain a deep, secure seat.

Training at Home

Even though barrel racing is all about speed, you can't start off training an inexperienced horse at a gallop. You have to start slow and gradually build from there. The best plan is to work with a trainer who is an experienced barrel racer.

Get your horse used to riding around the arena with the barrels set up. The first time you introduce your horse to the barrels should be at a walk only. If your horse is nervous or uncertain about them, you should dismount and walk him up to investigate the barrels. Let him sniff a barrel if he wants and look at it from all angles so he realizes there is nothing to be afraid of. Once he is accustomed to seeing them, you can walk him through the cloverleaf pattern. Since you can make either the right or left barrel your first barrel, experiment to find out which direction you are most comfortable going.

When he has walked the pattern several times without incident, cue him to trot and go through the pattern at this gait. Let your horse get to know the pattern at a trot before you ask for any more speed. It is much easier to control your horse and teach him to turn close to the barrel at a trot first before you speed up to the lope.

Instead of focusing just on the barrel, you want to look ahead through the turn. After your horse is confident in negotiating the pattern at slower speeds, you can begin asking him to go faster.

When you circle the barrel, you don't want to ride your horse directly at the barrel, but instead ride to a point about three feet to one side. You want the horse to slow down just before he reaches the barrel, about a horse length away, and start turning as you guide him around the barrel. You want the horse to almost roll back around the barrel on his hindquarters, not make a big circle around it. A wide circle takes more steps and more time. Your goal is to be both fast and precise, covering as little ground as possible in as short a time as you can. For that reason, your lines from barrel to barrel should be straight.

> It takes a great deal of practice to become a successful barrel racer. You need to be a brave and precise rider. Horse and rider must have trust and confidence in each other.

Don't just practice running barrels every time you ride, or your horse may get "sour" or nervous. Make sure to include trail riding and spend time out of the arena. It's good for both you and your horse to do other types of riding, not just speed events.

Pole Bending

Pole bending is another popular timed speed event that can often be found in high school and college rodeos, gymkhanas (mounted games) and horse shows. Picture a down-hill skier whipping back and forth between slalom poles and you have an idea of the challenge of pole bending.

A course of six poles is set up in a straight line with poles 21 feet apart. The first pole is 21 feet from the start/finish line. Poles, which are six feet tall, are made of PVC plastic and have a square base for support. The horse has a running start and must gallop in a straight line parallel to the poles. Upon reaching the first pole farthest from the starting point, the horse circles this pole and weaves his way back through the poles in a serpentine pattern. The horse circles the pole closest to the starting point and then weaves back through the pattern again. After circling the pole at the top of the pattern farthest from the starting line, the horse again races in a straight line parallel to the poles and back to the finish.

Pole bending requires a fast, athletic horse.

In pole bending, a time of 19 seconds is exceptional. A time of around 23 seconds is common for a rider who is not very experienced.

In barrel racing and pole bending, riders use a Western bridle and bit, along with a single-piece rein, known as a sport or game rein.

Horse and rider will be disqualified if they fail to follow the course. The rider can go to either the right or to the left of the first pole. The horse switches leads around each pole as he quickly changes directions.

Most riders keep both hands on the reins as their horse weaves through the pattern. When they make that final sharp turn and run for home, they often go to riding with one hand on the reins and the other hand on the horn for support.

Just as in barrel racing, one horse and rider team compete at a time, racing against the clock for the fastest winning time. An electronic timer or stopwatch is used to time each run down to a hundredth of a second. Time begins when the horse races across the start line and ends as soon as the horse's nose crosses the finish line.

The goal is to have the fastest time without knocking over any poles. There is a five second penalty for every pole knocked over during the run, but there is no penalty if the rider touches a pole and it remains standing. There is also a five second penalty if the rider's hat or helmet does not stay on the entire time she is in the arena.

The majority of pole benders ride in a barrel saddle because of its light weight and build. Any type of Western bridle and bit may be used and just as in barrel racing, riders use a single-piece game or sport rein.

As he turns each pole, the horse switches leads.

Stampede strings will help keep your hat on your head. Many riders wear knee guards as protection in case they bump a pole.

To compete in pole bending, your horse should:
- Be well trained and responsive to your cues
- Be athletic and good at changing leads
- Be familiar with the pattern

To compete in pole bending, you should:
- Have confidence in your horse and yourself
- Not be afraid of riding fast
- Feel comfortable with changing leads
- Have good control of your horse at all times
- Be familiar with the pattern

Because your horse will be moving fast and making sharp turns, he may need to wear leg protection.

Training at Home

To become successful at pole bending, your best option is to train with someone who is experienced in the sport. Because pole bending requires that the horse switch leads as he weaves through the poles, your horse needs to be very well trained and responsive.

Ride around the arena and let your horse get used to seeing the poles before you ride through them. Introduce your horse to the poles at a walk first. Let him sniff and investigate them if he likes.

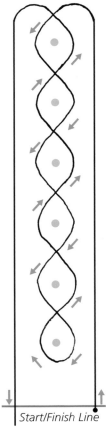

Example of a Pole bending pattern

Start/Finish Line

Your horse may need leg protection since he'll be making sharp turns.

Once he is accustomed to seeing them, you can walk him through the pattern. Since you can turn to either the right or left for the first pole, try both directions to see which is most comfortable for you and your horse.

Practice riding through the poles at a walk and then at the trot so the horse learns the pattern at a slower speed. Don't hurry to move on to a faster speed until your horse is responsive and weaving through the poles on his own. You want him to learn the pattern well at slower speeds before asking for a lope.

Unless your horse is much stronger on his right lead, most riders start the run on the horse's left lead. He should change leads as he weaves around each pole.

Horses usually catch on very quickly and change leads on their own as they weave through the pattern. Don't worry about going faster than a lope until the horse has mastered this. Once he has the pattern down

Get your horse used to going through the poles at a trot before you ask for speed.

at a lope, you can ask for more speed and fine-tune your run.

Your horse has to be athletic and agile, and you must be balanced and steady. It's important to sit deep and centered in the saddle to help your horse stay balanced around the poles.

Most riders start their run on the horse's left lead.

As much as you love pole bending, make sure you spend time doing other types of riding. If all you do is practice speed events, your horse will likely become excitable and want to gallop every time you saddle up. Add some fun riding time with friends and get out of the arena so your horse can relax and enjoy the ride as much as you do.

8. Reining

Reining is a popular Western riding competition that has origins in the world of the working American cowboy. Many of the moves seen in reining today – quick starts, spins, fast sprints and hard stops – are simply exaggerated versions of the maneuvers that cowboys used in their daily work.

Those cowboys relied on capable, athletic horses to help them do the job of herding, sorting, doctoring and branding cattle. Much of this tough work took place on the open range, far from corrals or fences, and it took a talented, agile horse to be in the right position at the right time to turn and move a cow.

The cowboy guided the horse using his legs and seat more than his hands on the reins. He needed a quick and responsive horse.

Today, reining is a popular equestrian discipline in many countries and competitors range in age from youth on up to senior riders. Many people consider reining the Western riding equivalent of dressage because horse and rider must perform specific maneuvers in a set pattern.

Any breed of horse may compete in reining, but stock horse breeds dominate the sport. The breed of horse doesn't matter, so long as the horse can execute the required maneuvers. One reason breeds such as the Quarter Horse excel in reining is because of their speed, agility and powerful hindquarters. Arabians and Morgans also compete in reining but are not seen as often as the stock horse breeds.

Reining is often considered the Western equivalent of dressage as horse and rider perform specific maneuvers in a designated pattern.

Unlike many horse show classes
where the crowd watches in
hushed silence, reining brings out
plenty of excitement. Spectators
at a reining event typically
whistle and shout to express
their appreciation when a horse
is performing well. An especially
powerful sliding stop or hard spin
will have the crowd clapping and
cheering enthusiastically.

As a sport, reining was first recognized by the American Quarter Horse Association in 1949. The National Reining Horse Association (NRHA), which is the main reining organization in the U.S. and Canada, was formed in 1966.

Reining is not just a North American sport, although many international competitions follow NRHA rules. Reining has spread around the world and was officially recognized by the Fédération Equestre Internationale (FEI) in 2000. The sport was added to the World Equestrian Games, held in Jerez, Spain, in 2002. The first FEI Reining World Championships were held in Italy in 2008, with competitors representing 16 different countries. Riders showing in an NRHA-approved event must be a member of the NRHA, or a European affiliate association. The horse must also have a competition license issued by the NRHA.

There are different divisions at reining shows and these may be broken down according to the experience of the horse and rider, among other criteria. Among standard classes are those for youth riders, professional and amateur riders, junior and senior horses, and horses of a specific age. There are also Open classes, which are open to all competitors.

Every pattern requires riding both fast and slow circles.

There are three divisions for youth riders: short stirrup (10 and under), 13 and under, and 14 to 18. For safety reasons, youth riders aren't allowed to compete on stallions.

One of the most popular classes for spectators is the Freestyle class, in which horse and rider perform reining maneuvers in a 3-1/2 minute routine set to music. Some contestants appear in costume and at times, even ride without a bridle. A certain number of maneuvers must be included in the performance and both technical merit and artistic impression are considered in the judging. It's not surprising that Freestyle classes draw some of the largest crowds at big reining events.

At a reining show, each contestant competes individually in an arena in front of several judges. All contestants in the same class must complete the same pattern. There are ten recognized reining patterns in the NRHA rule book. At an NRHA reining show, the show committee picks the patterns ahead of time and these are posted in The Reiner magazine, the official publication of the NRHA, and also before the classes at each show. At a breed show or an open show, the pattern will be posted the day of the show.

Flying lead changes should be smooth and timely with no change in speed.

Although patterns vary in difficulty, all patterns include seven to eight different maneuvers the horse must perform. It takes an average of 2-1/2 to three minutes for horse and rider to complete a pattern.

Let's take a look at the basic maneuvers:

Circles – Each pattern includes a number of circles and horses must execute both small circles at a slow lope, as well as large circles at a near gallop. The rider controls the speed and size of the circles, which should be perfectly round in shape.

Flying Lead Changes – Circles usually incorporate changes in direction that require flying lead changes, in which the horse changes leads without breaking gait. Judges

look to see that the horse changes leads completely in front and behind, and doesn't change too early or too late. The horse should not increase or decrease speed when changing leads.

Back Up – When backing, the horse must back up rapidly for at least ten feet. In addition to being quick, the back up must be smooth and in a straight line. The horse must stop when cued by the rider and then hesitate for a moment before going on to the next maneuver.

Rundown – This movement is required prior to a sliding stop. In a rundown, the horse must gallop down the long side of the arena, while staying at least 20 feet away from the fence.

Sliding Stop – Known as one of the signature maneuvers in reining, the sliding stop is a big crowd pleaser. The horse comes out of the rundown at a gallop and slides to a halt with his hindquarters tucked well underneath his body. The hind feet are planted and slide in the dirt, while the front feet continue to walk forward. The goal is to have a powerful stop in a straight line with the horse's position remaining unchanged.

Rollback – The horse goes into a rollback immediately after the sliding stop. In a rollback, the horse must execute a 180-degree turn following the stop and then break into a lope coming out of the turn. The maneuver should be fluid and smooth as the horse turns on his hindquarters.

The back up must be executed quickly and in a straight line.

The rundown is the gallop just before a sliding stop.

A good sliding stop is one of the most popular maneuvers in reining.

To perform a rollback after the sliding stop, the horse executes a 180-degree turn on the haunches and then moves directly into a lope coming out of this turn.

Spins – Also referred to as turnarounds, the spin is another crowd favorite. Every pattern requires at least one set of spins in both directions. Depending on the complexity of the pattern the horse may spin up to 4-1/4 full turns. Starting from a standstill, the horse turns around while keeping the inside hind leg planted in place. Judges look for smoothness and correctness in the spin; if a spin is done properly at high speed, this increases the score. To avoid being penalized for spinning too much or not enough, the horse must stop spinning in a designated spot. Overspinning more than a quarter-turn results in a zero score.

Hesitation – Between some maneuvers in the pattern the rider will ask the horse to hesitate, or pause, for a few seconds. This is routinely done after a spin. Judges look to see that the horse is not impatient or anxious during these brief periods before he's asked to go on to another maneuver.

Competition Time

Judges look for precision, speed, smoothness and cadence as they watch the horse's physical ability and his attitude throughout the pattern. It's not enough to perform the maneuvers correctly. The horse should also exhibit a willing and positive temperament, and not appear to require much assistance from the rider.

A fast spin is thrilling to watch as the horse turns around rapidly while remaining in the same place.

Reining requires that horse and rider be in close harmony. If not, the maneuvers will look rough or awkward, or the horse may appear unhappy or irritated, and this lowers the score.

Every horse starts with a score of 70 and judges then add or subtract points in increments of one-half point, one point, to one and a half points, depending on how the horse performs each of the maneuvers in that particular pattern. In addition, penalties ranging from one-half point to five points may be deducted. For example, trotting into a lead departure is a half point penalty; if the rider grabs the saddle with his free hand, this is a five point penalty. If the horse and rider go off pattern during competition, they are given a score of zero.

A score of 70 is considered average, meaning the horse made no serious mistakes, but neither did he perform exceptionally well. A score under 70 indicates that points were deducted because the horse performed maneuvers incorrectly and/or disobeyed or displayed poor attitude. A score above 70 means that some or all of the maneuvers were performed above average. A score of

plus one and a half on every maneuver is considered perfect and is rare.

Reining is meant to showcase the horse's ability, but the rider should also present a good appearance. The rider wears a Western hat and boots, jeans, and a long-sleeved shirt buttoned at the wrist. Chaps are a nice addition, but are not required. At NRHA events, a rider is allowed to wear a helmet instead of a Western hat, if he or she chooses.

Unlike some events where it's important to coordinate your attire with your horse's saddle pad, this is not a priority in reining. Your clothing and your horse's pad shouldn't clash, but they don't have to be precisely coordinated. Just be sure to present a clean, well-groomed overall picture. Women with long hair will look less distracting if their hair is pulled back into a braid or pony tail.

Riders compete in a reining saddle, which has forward hung stirrups that allow the rider to sit back and deep in the saddle during the hard stops and spins. A Western bridle is used and cannot have a noseband. Most bridles don't have a throatlatch, and one-ear and two-ear headstalls are acceptable. Riders usually ride with leather split reins, but romal reins may also be used. Tie-downs are not allowed. Some riders use a breast collar to help the saddle stay in place, but this is just a personal choice.

Most reining horses are shown in a curb bit, but there are also specific classes in which horses are shown in a snaffle bit or bosal hackamore. If riding with a curb bit, the rider should give rein cues with only one hand on the reins. Two hands are allowed when riding with a snaffle or bosal hackamore.

Most reining horses are shown in a Western curb bit.

Riders wear Western attire, which often includes chaps, and uses a reining saddle and a bridle without a noseband.

Certain curb bits are not allowed, and twisted curb chains cannot be used.

Riders should check the NRHA rule book to be certain what type of bits and curb chains are acceptable. This is important because at all NRHA events every rider's tack is checked by an equipment judge to be sure it's legal. At any show, a rider can talk with this person or any other judge to verify that the equipment they are using is legal and meets NRHA requirements.

Because of the complex maneuvers they must perform, reining horses often wear leg protection, such as boots or wraps, bell boots, and run-down boots.

> Reining horses wear special shoes, referred to as "slide plates" on their hind feet. These shoes are somewhat wider and longer than regular horseshoes and enhance the sliding effect when the horse stops.

Shoes on the reining horse's hind feet are longer and wider than standard shoes.

> **To compete in reining, your horse should:**
> - Be well trained and responsive to your cues
> - Know how to neck rein
> - Know how to execute the basic maneuvers
> - Be good at changing leads
> - Not speed up or slow down until you cue him

> **To compete in reining, you should:**
> - Feel confident and comfortable riding at all gaits
> - Have good position and control of your body in the saddle
> - Know how to execute basic maneuvers
> - Be familiar with patterns and reining rules
> - Know how to ask your horse to change leads
> - Be comfortable working at different speeds in all areas of the arena since you won't be working on the rail

Training at Home

If you want to get into the sport of reining, you'll need to find a knowledgeable trainer. Riders getting started in this event should look for an experienced reining horse. If you choose wisely, your horse can be a great teacher. Your trainer is a good person to help you find the right horse.

Before you take up reining you should be a competent rider and feel comfortable riding at all gaits. As a rider, you must have good position in the saddle at all times. For this reason, it's important to know basic equitation before you ever begin learning reining maneuvers. You need to master the discipline of controlling your body position so you can cue your horse correctly and not hinder him.

Even though many of the maneuvers performed in a reining pattern are things a horse does naturally, they are exaggerated. For example, every horse can spin around quickly, but when turned out by himself, a horse would have no reason to spin around rapidly several times in one spot. Horses love to run and you can often see them gallop along and then come to a quick stop out in the pasture. But in a reining pattern, the horse must gallop and then slide to a stop precisely when cued by the rider. You'll want to spend a lot of time practicing speeding up and slowing down without breaking gait, lead changes, rollbacks, spins and stopping.

A good trainer is essential if you want to excel in the sport of reining.

Many riders get dizzy when they start to learn spins. Your trainer can coach you on how to keep your head up and look for a spot in the arena to use as a focus point so you know when to cue your horse to stop spinning.

Reining is very close to dressage as it combines both collection and precision. Although reining involves speed, it isn't considered a speed event. It's all about control, precision and maintaining collection. Reining requires that you know where you should be in the arena at all times and are always thinking ahead to the next maneuver. One of the reasons so many riders have taken up reining is that it's not only a way to compete against other riders, but you are also competing against your last best score every time you enter the arena. There are always areas to improve and the thrill of performing well keeps riders coming back time after time. Riders who have switched to reining from other disciplines often say that reining is now the only style of riding they want to do. It's both challenging and rewarding to perfect the teamwork between you and your horse.

9. Cutting

There's no doubt that cutting is one of the fastest growing equestrian sports in the world. This quick-paced sport was born out of every day tasks that working cowboys performed on the open range.

In the United States in the 1800s, most grazing was considered "open range," meaning that there were few fences to keep cattle separated. Cattle belonging to one rancher would spread over miles of countryside to graze and intermingle with cattle belonging to another rancher.

Cattle were typically branded with their owner's distinctive brand, but as herds drifted, cows with different brands mixed together. It was up to the cowboys to separate them. This would usually take place in the spring and fall when cowboys would round up the herds and then separate them out according to brand.

Even when cattle didn't mix with other herds, it was often necessary to separate a cow or calf out for doctoring or branding. That's when a horse came in handy. American cowboys had a string,

or group, of horses to do all the hard work they had to accomplish. Some horses were better suited for certain tasks than others. One of the most valuable horses in the string was the cutting horse. This was the mount a cowboy chose to ride when separating cattle.

What made the cutting horse special was his unique ability to "read" a cow. He would watch closely and follow every move a cow made. He had natural "cow sense" and seemed to know instinctively what to do. His talents helped the cowboy cut a cow out from the herd, and his athletic ability kept that cow from rejoining the group.

Cowboys were proud of their horses and when a chance arose to prove who had the best horse, these men were sure to show up.

A good cutting horse has the ability to "read" a cow.

A good cutting horse often appears to "mirror" the cow's movements.

A good cutting horse makes a tough job look easy. His gaze remains focused on the cow as he pivots back and forth on his hindquarters, and dashes to one side or the other, all the while keeping the cow separated from the herd.

The first advertised cutting contest took place in 1898 in Haskell, Texas, at the Cowboy Reunion. The event was well advertised and nearly 15,000 people attended. Eleven riders entered in hopes of winning the $150 prize, which was considered a large amount in those days.

One of those contestants was Sam Graves who had a 22-year-old horse by the name of Old Hub. The senior citizen horse was actually retired from working, but his owner decided to take him out of retirement for this one contest. Old Hub didn't let Graves down. He proved himself the best of all the horses entered and won the prize.

Cutting contests became so popular that in 1946, a group of horsemen met in Texas and formed the National Cutting Horse Association (NCHA) to set standard rules for these competitions. The first show was held that same year in Dublin, Texas.

Cutting was once part of a cowboy's normal routine and often he didn't have a fancy, well-bred horse. That has changed through the years as the popularity of cutting has grown.

Today's cutting horses are carefully bred for bloodlines that are known for their cow sense and athletic ability. The sport has grown dramatically. In fact, cutting has now spread to about two dozen countries around the world with annual prize money totaling many millions of dollars.

In addition to the NCHA in the United States, there are cutting associations and competitions in Europe, Australia and Canada. Cutting is a popular youth event and young riders compete to win prizes and even scholarships. Youth compete in cutting events in two divisions: Junior, which is 13 and under, and Senior for riders age 14 to 18.

Reins are held with one hand only; the other hand holds the horn for stability.

What It Takes

Although different breeds are certainly welcome, the Quarter Horse is most commonly seen in cutting events. The breed's versatility, athleticism and natural cow sense make him a natural in the sport, and certain bloodlines are bred specifically for cutting.

Most cutting horses are rather small, but extremely agile and quick. A horse with a high ability to work a cow is often described as "cat-like" because of the way the horse almost "crouches" in front of the cow while working, and also because the horse is so light on his feet.

At a cutting competition, the horse and rider must select and separate a cow out of a group of cattle and drive it to the center of the arena or pen. Because cattle are herd animals, they always try to return to the group. It's the horse's job to keep that from happening.

It's important to know about cattle because the cow you select can help or hinder the scoring. An energetic, alert cow allows the horse to show what he can do, but a calm, quiet cow won't be much of a challenge.

Reins are held with one hand only. The rider can use his legs to direct his horse but isn't allowed to guide his horse with the reins once the cow is selected from the herd. Instead, he puts his hand down on the horse's neck or the pommel of the saddle and keeps the reins loose.

The rider must sit deep in the saddle and keep one hand on the horn of the saddle to stay steady as the horse cuts rapidly back

The rider selects a cow to drive out of the herd.

and forth. The rider's back should be loose and relaxed, not straight. Some people call this the "cutter's slump" because the rider is actually sitting back on his pockets instead of straight up in the saddle.

There are four "turn back" riders in the arena to assist during the cutting. Two of these riders are called "herd holders" and have the task of holding the herd together. The other two riders are on the side of the arena farthest from the herd. Their job is to keep the cow in front of the cutting horse by not allowing the cow to run down the arena away from the herd and toward the judging stand. These riders aren't part of the scoring, but are only there to help. It's each exhibitor's responsibility to arrange for turn back riders.

There is a 2-1/2 minute time limit, during which the horse separates two to three cattle.

Time starts once the horse crosses a line about 50 feet in front of the herd. As soon as the cow turns away and stops trying to re-join the herd, the rider can lift his reins. This lets the horse know he can stop working that cow. Horse and rider then re-enter the herd of cattle to cut out a new cow.

The horse is judged on his ability to keep the cow from returning to the herd, and is also scored on his cow sense, attentiveness and courage. The judges like to see deter-mination and style in the horse.

Judges award points to each contestant based on a scale ranging from 60 to 80. Each horse enters the arena with a score of 70, which is considered average. Depending on how well the horse works the cattle, points are added or subtracted so the score goes up or down from 70. The highest score wins.

While cutting, the reins should be loose and the hand holding the reins must not be used to direct the horse.

If a cow gets past the horse and returns to the herd, this is called a "lost cow" and results in penalty points.

To compete in cutting, your horse should:
- Be well trained and responsive to your cues
- Be fit and in good shape
- Have "cow savvy" and be used to cattle
- Know how to track and "read" a cow
- Know how to stop, back and turn well
- Stay parallel to the cow while working, not getting ahead of or behind the cow

Horses are ridden in a cutting saddle, which has a tall horn the rider holds with his free hand for stability. Cutting saddles have a flatter seat than other Western saddles and the stirrups are hung farther forward than a regular Western saddle in order to help the rider maintain a deep seat. A back girth helps keep the saddle in place.

The horse may be shown in a Western bridle with a curb-style bit or a hackamore. The headstall may not have a noseband of any sort and no tie-downs are allowed.

When competing, riders wear a long-sleeved shirt (button or snaps) with a collar, jeans, Western hat and boots, and chaps.

To compete in cutting you should:
- Be comfortable riding a horse that will move quickly and make sudden sharp turns
- Be familiar enough with cattle to understand how they move and react
- Know where the horse should be in relation to the cow
- Rely mainly on your legs and seat instead of your hands to communicate with your horse
- Be familiar with the rules of cutting if you intend to compete

Plenty of riding outside the arena will help keep your horse fit.

Learning to Cut

To properly learn this exciting sport, it's important to work with a trainer who is respected and experienced in cutting. In addition to knowing the ins and outs of cutting, a good trainer will also have the cattle necessary for you and your horse to learn. Groups of cattle must be rotated on a regular basis because cattle will get sour or quiet after they have been used for a while.

Many horse owners don't have access to their own cattle at home. Although you definitely need to practice working on live cattle, you can also do a lot with your horse by training on a mechanical cow or a flag, which is a piece of fabric or material. Just

Your horse must use his powerful hind end to work the cow properly.

as it sounds, a mechanical cow is a fake fiberglass cow, or a blow-up inflatable "cow" that is mounted on a pulley system in the arena to move back and forth.

The pulley system is controlled by pedals. You need someone else to work the pedals that move the flag or "cow" back and forth so you and your horse can work the flag or cow. Both objects give the horse something to focus on as he learns to follow it, stop and turn back in the other direction. The speed and direction of these objects can also be controlled, unlike a live cow.

Of course, a real cow has a mind of its own and that is what makes cutting such an exciting challenge. The flag or mechanical cows are great for practicing, but there's nothing like a real live cow stopping, turning and making a run for it to bring out the best in a talented horse.

Everything about cutting requires that your horse work off his hindquarters, so it's important that he knows how to back up, stop and perform turna-

rounds and rollbacks. Your horse should be very responsive and understand these maneuvers before you ever start practicing on cattle.

Working with his powerful hind end underneath him allows the horse to turn and move quickly. Your trainer will encourage you to back your horse before he stops and changes directions. This will help keep your horse working off his hindquarters. He must also know how to neck rein, since you ride with only one hand.

Even if your horse is bred for cutting, he still needs to be introduced to cattle and be taught to work them.

The horse's focus should always be on the cow.

The first few times you ride your horse around cattle, it's a wise idea to have someone else on a horse that is experienced and quiet with cows. This will help your horse realize he doesn't have to be afraid and help him gain confidence. Being around cattle will help both you and your horse understand how they act and react.

Riding along behind one or two calm cows is a good way to give your horse his first introduction to cattle. Once your horse is comfortable with this, your trainer will start letting you work with one quiet cow in the arena.

A good cutting horse must read the cow and think about what he needs to do to control the cow's movements. Your job as a rider is just to help your horse be in the right position to work the cow. Any time you are working cattle, your horse should be looking towards the cow so he can keep on eye on the cow at all times. He should respond to what the cow does. If the cow moves left, your horse should do the same. If the cow spins and goes the other direction, your horse should do the same.

Some of the most thrilling moments in cutting happen when the cow is trying to return to the herd and the horse is rapidly shifting back and forth to prevent this. The horse's front end is often lower than his hindquarters as he moves gracefully. It's all up to the horse at this point; the rider is just along for the ride!

The rider should sit deep in the saddle with one hand on the horn to help stay stable during the horse's quick movements.

In the beginning when your horse is learning what is expected of him you may work with cattle almost every day. Once he's experienced at cutting, you won't need to work with cattle so often. If you are going to a show, your trainer will probably have you work cows two or three times that week. Otherwise, most of your riding is to keep your horse fit and responsive to you.

Cutting is demanding, physical work, so it's very important that your horse be fit and in shape. You will want to ride regularly and include plenty of loping and/or extended trotting so he's in good condition. It's a good idea to include trail riding so your horse is getting the exercise he needs and isn't always in the arena.

When you are in the show pen at a cutting, you must rely on your legs and seat to guide your horse, so start getting in the habit of using them more and your hands less. Make it a habit to ride with one hand since you can only use one hand when you are competing.

You will need a cutting saddle, which is designed to help keep you sitting deep in the saddle – something you will definitely need when your horse really starts to move! When cutting, you always have one hand on the horn for stability. It's natural to want to pull the horn to hold on, but this will actually bring you forward in the saddle and put you off balance. Instead, you'll want to push against the horn to help you sit deeper and have more stability.

You can use a variety of different bits for cutting; your trainer will help you decide which bit is best for your particular horse. Hackamores and tie-downs are not allowed when competing. You'll use basic split leather reins and ride with just one hand.

Boots will help protect your horse's legs while cutting.

Depending on the length of your arm, you may be more comfortable resting your hand on the pommel of the saddle. You can also rest your hand on the horse's neck in front of the saddle. Picking up your hand to steer the horse while he is working a cow is a penalty, so get in the habit of "dropping your hand" and keeping it still until your horse is finished with the cow.

Your horse should wear boots on his front legs for protection. Many riders also put protective boots on their horse's back legs. Some horses also wear bell boots over their hooves to offer more protection.

10. Trail Riding

A brisk trot on a crisp autumn day… carefree laughter with friends as you ride along a shady trail… an exhilarating gallop across a grassy meadow. Some of the best memories with your horse can be made on trail rides.

Whether you just want to ride for fun or are working toward serious competition, trail riding should have a place in your routine. Even professional trainers like to use trail riding to keep their horses mentally fresh and to prevent boredom from riding in an arena too much.

Remember that even though no judge's eyes will be watching when you're riding on the trail, good position and proper horsemanship are important because they help you control your horse. When you have control of your horse, you will also have a safer ride and be able to enjoy your time on the trail.

> A trail riding horse should be well trained and gentle. You want a horse that is responsive to your cues and doesn't have bad habits, like jigging along or hurrying home. He should be easy to ride in company with other horses or alone.

Trail riding is a great way to enjoy your horse and your friends at the same time.

If this is your first horse, don't be afraid of buying an older horse. It's a mistake to get a young, green (inexperienced) horse if you are a novice rider.

Stay Safe!

No one really cares what attire you ride in, but it should be safe and sensible. It's always a good idea to wear a helmet when trail riding.

For safety reasons, ride in a proper boot with a heel. Don't ride in sneakers or any shoe or boot without a heel, as your foot might slide through the stirrup and get caught.

It's best to ride with someone else on the trail so you aren't alone if something happens. Be sure to let someone know where you are going and when you plan to be back so they can be aware if you don't show up.

If your horse hasn't done much trail riding, your first times on the trail should be with other horses that are quiet and experienced. Your horse will remember these rides, so make them positive.

If you plan to do much trotting or loping, this should be done earlier in your ride before you are heading home. The last part of your ride home should always be at a walk. If you get into the habit of going quickly toward home, your horse will develop a tendency to rush back, and this can be dangerous.

If you carry a cell phone for emergencies when trail riding, make sure it's attached to your body, not to your saddle. This way if you get separated from your horse for any reason, you have the phone with you. Be courteous! Set your phone to vibrate so it doesn't ring and startle your horse or other riders' horses when trail riding.

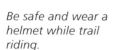

Be safe and wear a helmet while trail riding.

Don't leave good manners behind when you ride! When you are riding with a group and not everyone wants to trot or lope, you should drop back and/or off to the side a good distance if you want to ride at a faster pace. Don't just ride ahead of the group and then start trotting or loping because that will make their horses upset and they'll want to catch up.

When riding with other riders, always make sure the group is prepared for a change of pace. You can communicate by talking or use hand signals if in a large group to let others know if you are speeding up or slowing down.

It's important to keep a safe distance between horses, both in front and back and on the side. Keep a horse length's distance between horses, or about eight to ten feet. This will help prevent riders and other horses from getting kicked. Always be aware of the horses and riders around you. If a horse is pinning his ears or wringing his tail, he may be about to kick, so stay a safe distance away.

Be polite on the trail! If you are passing another rider or a group of riders, speak up if you are approaching from behind so they know you are coming. Always pass at a walk so you don't frighten other horses.

If you come up on a spooky obstacle that scares your horse, don't be afraid to dismount and walk him past it. If you feel safer this way, by all means, step down and lead your horse by the scary thing. This can give him confidence and prevent an accident if he were to bolt. Just be sure that you don't put him between you and the object or he might jump onto you if he spooks.

To keep your horse (or yourself) from accidentally getting kicked, always keep a distance of eight to ten feet between horses.

If your horse is scared about something he sees on the trail, dismount and lead him past it several times. Once he's quiet and accepting, you can remount and ride by it again just to show him the scary thing is really harmless.

Let your horse get a good look at the obstacle from both sides so he realizes it won't hurt him. He may snort and blow, but allow him to sniff it if he wants. Remember that horses are prey animals and it is their instinct to run first and think later. That big dark rock under a tree along the trail may look like a bear or a crouching lion to him!

Once the horse has investigated the scary thing with you leading him on the ground and accepts that it is harmless, then you can remount. Ride back by the obstacle several times from both directions. This will help build his confidence in himself and his trust in you.

Some riders get in the habit of letting their horses eat along the trail, but this isn't wise. You have much less control if your horse's head is down and he's munching grass. It's also rude to other riders around you. When your horse has his head down trying to eat, he won't be paying attention to where he's going, and he might trip or stumble.

If you want to let your horse graze or give him treats, save this for after the ride when he's untacked and relaxed. Don't let him eat while riding on the trail.

Let your horse eat when you get back to the trailer or home… not on the trail!

Trail Riding Exercises

Did you know that you are always teaching your horse? Even when you might think you're just out for a casual trail ride with friends, your horse is still learning.

If you let him get away with things – such as grabbing bites of grass or not responding when you cue him – you can be sure he'll try this again. Horses will get away with whatever they can, and they will test you to see if you really mean what you say with your cues and commands. A responsible rider is always consistent. If you are consistent your horse will look to you to be the leader. If you are unsure and inconsistent, your horse will think it's up to him to be the leader.

A good way to reinforce that you are the leader and still have a pleasant time is to add exercises to your trail ride. This gives your horse a task to accomplish, makes him pay closer attention to you, and will help improve your horsemanship skills.

Here are some exercises you can practice on the trail:

Vary the Pace

A trot is not just a trot. You can add spice to your ride by varying the pace of different gaits. On your next trail ride, experiment to see how you can vary the pace of the three common gaits – walk, trot and lope.

See how slow and how fast your horse can walk without breaking into a trot. Then vary the pace of the trot. First ask for a slow jog. Then use your seat and legs to ask your horse to quicken to a medium trot. Next ask him to extend that trot without breaking into a lope. If you are comfortable at the lope, you can also try varying the speed at this gait, going from a slow, collected lope to a regular lope and then to a hand gallop.

To keep it interesting, vary the pace throughout your ride. Just remember not to trot or lope when you are almost back to the stable, otherwise your horse will anticipate this and start hurrying home.

Circles & Serpentines

You can do some of the same exercises you practice in the ring or arena on the trail. Just make sure the footing is safe and you have enough room.

Instead of riding straight down the middle of the trail, use your legs to cue your horse to the left and right and wind your way along the trail in a serpentine. You can do this at a walk and at a trot.

If you reach a wider place in the trail, trot in a circle to one direction. Make a figure-eight through the middle of the circle and trot in the other direction. Then continue on your ride. You can also trot circles around a tree. Vary the size of the circles and the speed of your trot to add challenge to this exercise.

Trotting circles around trees along the trail is a good way to practice controlling your horse.

Uphill & Down

If there are hills where you ride, this is great exercise for your horse and also good practice for you.

When you ride uphill, you should stay balanced in the center of your saddle, but lean your upper body slightly forward. Your legs should be directly underneath you just as when you are riding on the flat; don't let them move back or forward. Keep your hands forward to give your horse enough slack in the reins that you don't snatch his mouth. Look ahead up the hill instead of looking down as this will put you off balance.

Some horses want to run uphill because that makes it easier for them, but this is not the

On a gradual uphill incline, just lean your upper body slightly forward, but stay balanced and in the center of the saddle seat.

wise thing to do. You should always be in control and your horse should walk up the hill unless you ask him for another gait.

When riding downhill, you should stay balanced and centered in the saddle with your upper body leaning just slightly back in the saddle, but not dramatically. Your feet and legs should be slightly in front of the horse's girth. Hold your hands a little higher than usual; this will encourage the horse to get his hindquarters underneath him more as he goes down the hill. Don't lean forward or look down.

Always ride downhill at a walk. It's easy for a horse to stumble or even fall if he is going downhill fast.

If the hill is very steep, it will be easier on your horse if you take the hill at a diagonal instead of going straight down. Zigzag back and forth down the hill.

Water Crossing

Crossing streams and creeks can be great fun, but it can also be frightening for your horse if he hasn't done this before.

If you know you are going to ride where you'll cross water for the first time, be sure to go with other riders whose horses are experienced and will cross without trouble. This will give your horse confidence as he can watch and follow their actions.

Of course, this also applies in the negative. If you ride with someone whose horse acts up and refuses to cross the water, your horse may do the same and put up a fight. If you are uncertain or nervous, these feelings will transfer to your horse and he will become anxious. Don't start out trying to cross water if you aren't sure of yourself. You have to be confident and give your horse consistent cues in order for him to go through water.

When riding downhill, stay centered in your saddle, but lean your upper body slightly back to help your horse stay balanced.

A shallow puddle is great for introducing your horse to crossing water.

Always make sure you know how deep the water is before going in, and take off any tie-downs or martingales before crossing water. These devices are meant to keep a horse's head down, and if he should hit a deep spot he could drown if he can't raise his head.

For the first water crossing, a stream or big puddle just a few inches deep is ideal. Most horses will cross water if given the time to relax so they realize it won't hurt them.

Ride your horse up to the edge of the water and stop him. Allow him to drop his head and sniff the water. Praise him by stroking his neck and talking to him. Keep him facing towards the water and don't let him turn around.

Cue him with your legs and seat to take another step forward. You may have to do this several times before he puts a foot in the water, but be sure to praise him every time he takes even one step forward.

Once your horse has investigated the water, let another experienced horse ride on and cross it so your horse can follow.

Don't stop in the middle of the water because many horses like to drop and roll. If your horse starts pawing, that is a sign he may be about to go down and roll, so keep him moving!

Once you cross the water, praise your horse. Let him stand and relax a minute so he realizes he did the right thing. Then turn around and cross the water again a few times so he understands it's not a big deal.

A good trail horse should stand quietly while you mount from either side... even the right side.

Although most riders always mount and dismount from the horse's left side, there is no rule that says it must be done this way. You should practice getting on and off from both sides. You never know when you might find yourself in a situation, such as on a narrow trail, where you might need to mount or dismount from the right side.

Competitive Endurance Riding

Did you know you can enjoy trail riding in a competitive setting? Many riders compete in rides sanctioned by the North American Trail Ride Conference (NATRC). Rides may range from 15 to 90 miles, covering from one to three days.

Founded in 1961, the NATRC has helped make competitive trail riding an extremely popular equine activity. The sport promotes good horsemanship, along with proper training and conditioning of horses for trail riding. Participating in the rides is an ideal way to learn how to condition your horse, manage his health and fitness, and confront the challenges of different terrain and weather on the trail.

You can ride any breed of horse so long as it has the necessary stamina and hardiness. Winners of past rides include many different breeds, including Arabians and part-Arabs, Missouri Fox Trotters, American Saddlebreds, Appaloosas, Morgans, Tennessee Walking Horses, Mustangs, mules and other breeds.

In the Junior division, riders aged 10 through 17 can compete on competitive trail rides of varying distances.

Horse and rider cover the designated trail at their own pace, and must stop at mandatory vet checks along the way. Here, the pulse and respiration of each horse is checked, as well as the horse's soundness. There are at least two vet checks every day, or more, depending on the length of the ride. If a horse does not pass the vet check, that horse and rider are not allowed to finish the ride.

Horses are judged on physical condition, soundness, trail ability and manners. Riders are judged on grooming of their horse, in-hand presentation, tack and equipment, trail equitation, trail care, trail safety and courtesy, and stabling. Each competitor gets a scorecard at the end of the ride, showing how that horse and rider scored.

In Conclusion

By now you've probably decided which Western riding events are most appealing to you. As you continue to practice and learn, you and your horse will do better in competition. Don't be discouraged when you're starting out. Remember, it takes months and years to excel in any riding discipline, and some are tougher than others.

Get ready to enjoy the excitement and challenge of competing. But most of all have fun becoming partners with your horse. The more time you spend together, the closer you will become and the better you'll understand him. All the blue ribbons and trophies in the world don't compare to truly having a great relationship with an equine friend you can trust and rely upon.

Riding safely and having fun with your horse should always be your priority. Don't get so focused on mastering an event or style of riding that you forget this. It's easy to get bogged down in practicing and drilling on a maneuver or lesson you're trying to learn. Never forget that the reason you began riding in the first place was your passion for horses.

Horses are amazing partners. If we treat them right and communicate with them in ways they understand, they will do things for us they would never do on their own.

Respect your horse. Don't expect him to learn new things in just one or two lessons. Be kind and patient. Make it a point to be the type of rider your horse can trust and depend on.

Keep learning, stay safe, and may you always ride a horse that makes you smile!